KENTUCKY

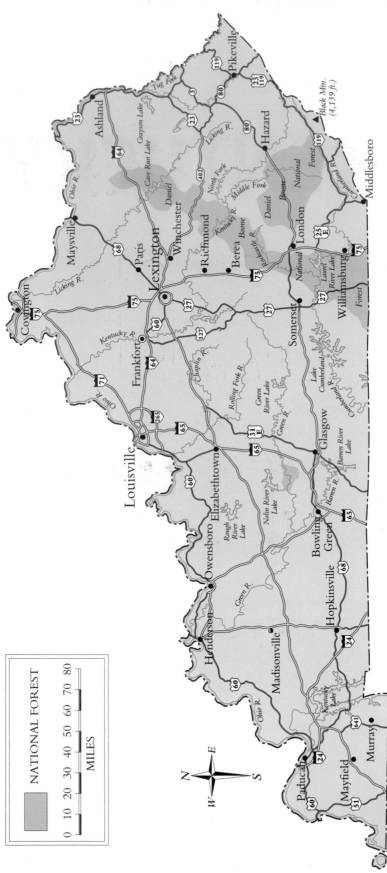

KENTUCKY BY ROAD

CELEBRATE THE STATES
KENTUCKY

Tracy Barrett

BENCHMARK BOOKS

MARSHALL CAVENDISH
NEW YORK

For Laura, Patrick, and Josh

Benchmark Books
Marshall Cavendish Corporation
99 White Plains Road
Tarrytown, New York 10591-9001

Copyright © 1999 by Marshall Cavendish Corporation

Library of Congress Cataloging-in-Publication Data
Barrett, Tracy, date
Kentucky / Tracy Barrett.
p. cm. — (Celebrate the states)
Summary: An overview of the geography, history, people, and customs of the Bluegrass State.
ISBN 0-7614-0657-3 (lib. Bdg.)
1. Kentucky—Juvenile literature. [1. Kentucky.] I. Title. II. Series.
F451.3.B37 1999 976.9—dc21 97-38589 CIP AC

Maps and graphics supplied by Oxford Cartographers, Oxford, England

Photo research by Candlepants Incorporated

Cover photo: The Image Bank / Walter Ioss Jr.

The photographs in this book are used by permission and through the courtesy of: *Adam Jones*: 6-7, 10-11, 15, 17, 21, 22(bottom), 23, 24, 48-49, 57, 59, 77, 96-97, 100, 108, 109, 117, 126, back cover. *The Image Bank*: Gary Cralle, 16, 107; Gary S. Chapman, 62-63. *Photo Researchers, Inc.*: Jeff Lepore, 19, 121; Leonard Lee Rue, 22(top); Frederica Georgia, 76; E. Hanumantha Rao, 120. *The Filson Club Historical Society, Louisville, Kentucky*: 26-27, 43, 44. *Collection of New York Historical Society*: 29. *The Anschutz Collection*: 32. *Dept. Of Library Special Collection, Western Kentucky University*: 35, 52. *Archives and Special Collections Berea College*: 39. *J. Winston Coleman Photographic Collection, Transylvania University Library*: 41. *University of Kentucky Libraries*: 45. *Courier-Journal*: 46. *Gene Boaz*: 55, 61, 67, 69, 78-79, 103, 106, 111, 114, 124, 136. *Corbis-Bettmann* 71, 81, 128. *UPI/Corbis-Bettmann*: 84, 90, 93. *Archive Photos*: 82, 83, 87, 89, 94, 129, 131(top), 131(bottom), 132, 133. *Archive Photos/Frank Driggs Collections*: 85. *Archive Photos/Darlene Hammond*: 88. *Kentucky Department of Travel*: 72. *Raymond Bial*: 74, 105, 112. *Office of the Secretary of State of Kentucky*:116.

Printed in Italy

1   3   5   6   4   2

CONTENTS

KENTUCKY IS...

Kentuckians are friendly . . .

"You know you're in Kentucky, because every door is open to a stranger."   —Author Bobbie Ann Mason

. . . and they are tough.

"A Kentuckian kneels to none except his God, and always dies facing his enemy."
    —Mexican War hero William Logan Crittenden, on refusing
        to kneel or wear a blindfold when executed in 1850

Kentuckians love their state . . .

"When the Kentuckian encounters dangers of battle, or of any kind, when he is even on board a foundering ship, his last exclamation is: Hurrah for old Kentucky."
                                                        —Irish visitor Timothy Flint, 1831

"When a man from Nebraska, say, or Michigan, speaks of his country the chances are that he is thinking of the Union. Nine times out of ten a Kentuckian, using the same language, will have in his brain a picture of that particular part of Kentucky wherein he was born. Not that the Kentuckian is less patriotic than the Michigan man or less nationally minded than the Nebraskan. It's just the way he's built, that's all. . . . He's different and he's glad of it."
                                                        —Humorist Irvin S. Cobb, 1924

"If these United States can be called a body, Kentucky can be called its heart."   —Author Jesse Stuart

. . . and its beauty.

"Kentucky is a second paradise."   —Pioneer Daniel Boone

"Heaven is a Kentucky kind of place."
    —Anonymous preacher, 1800s

Kentucky has also sometimes been a bloody place. From conflicts among the Indians through battles between settlers and Native Americans, the Civil War, the feuds of eastern Kentucky, the Black Patch War, and modern racial clashes, Kentucky has seen more than its share of violence. But Kentuckians have worked hard for peace, and their efforts are paying off. They now have a crime rate below the national average. Today, Kentucky is a busy, productive state, with one of the best school systems in the country, thriving industry, and proud citizens. Come explore the Bluegrass State and see why its people have worked so hard to make the state a peaceful, as well as beautiful, place to live.

1 A KENTUCKY KIND OF PLACE

Although the name "Kentucky" certainly comes from a Native American word, no one is precisely sure which one. It may come from a Cherokee word, *Kentahteh*, meaning "land of tomorrow" or "meadow land." One legend—that the word means "dark and bloody ground," after a particularly brutal Indian battle—is probably untrue.

Some people, perhaps thinking of its violent past, say that Kentucky is shaped like a dented shield. Others think that it looks like a camel lying down. Kentucky's southern border is flat, and its northern edge rises to a jagged peak, just like one of the mountains in the state's eastern section. In the east, Kentucky measures 180 miles north to south, while in the west, it narrows to a mere 40 miles.

Kentucky is bordered on the north by Ohio, Indiana, and Illinois; on the west by Missouri; on the south by Tennessee; and on the east by Virginia and West Virginia. One part of Kentucky can't be reached by land except from another state: eighteen square miles that lie inside a loop of the Mississippi River must be entered from Tennessee.

THE BIRTH OF KENTUCKY

Hundreds of millions of years ago, an ocean covered what is now Kentucky. The Appalachian Mountains began rising out of this

LAND AND WATER

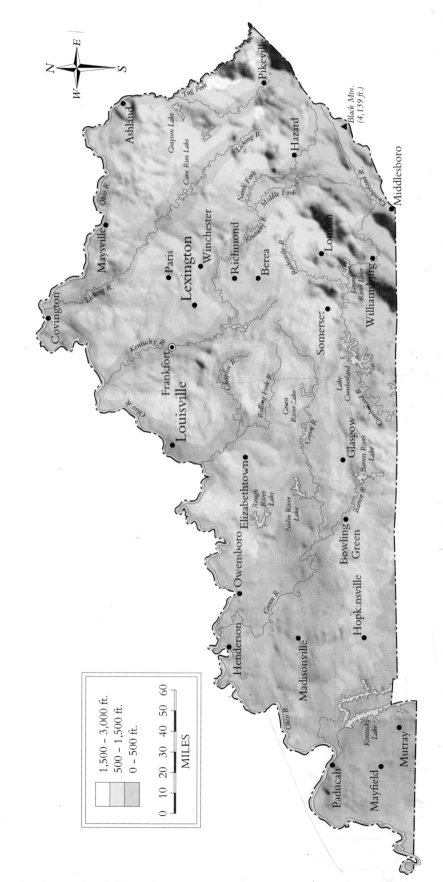

Ashland

Pikeville

Tug Fork

Grayson Lake

Licking R.

Hazard

Black Mtn.
(4,139 ft.)

Cane Run Lake

Maysville

North Fork

Middle Fork

Middlesboro

Ohio R.

Cumberland R.

Covington

Licking R.

Paris

Lexington

Winchester

Richmond

Berea

Kentucky R.

London

Rockcastle R.

Williamsburg

Laurel River Lake

Kentucky R.

Frankfort

Somerset

Louisville

Chaplin R.

Rolling Fork R.

Green River Lake

Green R.

Lake Cumberland

Ohio R.

Cumberland R.

Elizabethtown

Rough River Lake

Nolin River Lake

Glasgow

Barren River Lake

Owensboro

Bowling Green

Barren R.

Henderson

Green R.

Hopkinsville

Madisonville

Ohio R.

Paducah

Kentucky Lake

Mayfield

Murray

| 1,500 – 3,000 ft. |
| 500 – 1,500 ft. |
| 0 – 500 ft. |

MILES

0 10 20 30 40 50 60

ocean 230 million years ago, as large plates of land pushed slowly against each other and crumpled into mountains. Toward the west, the plates sloped off into what is now flat farmland. In the eastern part of the state, the broken edges of the plates gradually wore away into odd rounded hills which are now called the Knobs. After the mountains rose and the ocean poured into what is now the Atlantic, huge forests grew. The enormous coal deposits in eastern Kentucky are the remnants of this swampy forest. Even after decades of mining, about 60 billion tons of coal remain in the ground there.

The receding sea left behind a wealth of salt. Prehistoric mammals were attracted to these salt deposits, as are deer and bears today. Big Bone Lick in northern Kentucky is named for the fossilized skeletons of mastodons and mammoths—giant elephant-like beasts—that came to lick the salt and got stuck in the mud. Native Americans and early European explorers made furniture from the bones. Future U.S. president Thomas Jefferson was fascinated by the fossils and took some home to Virginia.

FOUR KENTUCKIES

Geographically, Kentucky can be divided into four regions. In the east, the beautiful Appalachian Mountains provide a scenic backdrop of stunning streams and forests. Rivers such as the Cumberland and the Big Sandy wind their way through the mountains, often passing through deep ravines. Small towns and coal mines pepper the east's narrow valleys and steep hills.

The Bluegrass Region is named for the grass that covers the

The Cumberland River cuts a wide swath through the Appalachian Mountains.

north-central part of the state. There, large horse farms spread across gentle hills, and Louisville, the state's largest city, sits on the bank of the Ohio River. South-central Kentucky is filled with fertile farmland, fascinating caves, and lovely lakes. As the state flattens away to the west, the landscape opens up.

WATER AND WEATHER

Kentucky is watered by 13,000 miles of streams and rivers. Among the fifty states, only huge Alaska has more miles of running water.

Horse farms blanket Kentucky's Bluegrass Region.

Kentucky provides rafters with plenty of impressive scenery.

The mighty Ohio River, which runs along Kentucky's northern border, is wide and calm. Most of Kentucky's major cities, such as Louisville, Owensboro, Covington, and Paducah, grew up along the Ohio, which was easy to navigate.

But many of the state's smaller streams rush down hillsides and through narrow gorges. "This is a great state for white-water," says enthusiastic visitor Greg Giles. "If you like exciting rapids, you can find them, or you can paddle a canoe down a quiet stream. They have some of everything here." At the bottom of Kentucky's rivers you can sometimes find geodes, round rocks that when broken open reveal "a whole crystal world," recalls former Kentuckian Miriam Moore.

Many of Kentucky's rivers are fed by underground streams. These streams have carved out at least two thousand caves, the most of any state in the country. Kentucky's Mammoth Cave is the largest known cave system in the world, but most of the state's caves are small. Still, Kentuckians have taken advantage of them. Milbrey Dugger's grandfather lived on a farm near Cave City during the Civil War. "Pappa told me that during the war, soldiers would sweep through the countryside and steal everything they could find," she recalls. "The children were posted as lookouts, and whenever they heard of any soldiers in the area, they would take the cattle and horses into the caves and hide them there until the coast was clear."

Kentucky has a temperate climate. In winter, the temperature often drops below freezing, while summers are hot and humid, especially in low-lying areas. Becky Ray, who grew up on a farm near Louisville in the 1950s, remembers the summer heat as being unbearable in her old house, which had a tin roof. "We had electricity, but no running water," she recalls. "But it was so hot that we got an air conditioner even before we had water in the house." Kentucky averages forty-eight inches of rain each year. Snow falls throughout the state, with the mountains receiving the most, usually about fifteen inches each winter.

THE ENDANGERED BAT

Kentucky's intriguing caves attract throngs of visitors each year. At first glance these caves may seem deserted, but in truth they are home to many varieties of wildlife. One of these is the gray bat.

Bats are shy creatures. They do not fly into people's hair or attack visitors to their caves. The danger in caving is not from the bats, but to them. As visitors flood into caves, the bats' roosting areas are disturbed. Some bats stop reproducing or abandon their babies when people come too near. Also, pesticide use and land development have changed the caves' environment and reduced the population of the insects the bats prey on.

All these factors have combined to put the gray bat on the endangered species list. Cave visitors are encouraged to be careful around the bats' roosting sites and to keep out of the caves while the bats are there. In some places, putting fences at cave entrances has helped restore the gray bat population.

KENTUCKY WILDLIFE

Because Kentucky has both mountains and plains, a large variety of plants and animals can live there. Thick forests, which cover half the state, are full of hardwood trees such as elm, ash, hickory, maple, and oak and softwoods such as cypress, cedar, hemlock, and pine. A tremendous assortment of trees thrives in Kentucky— in all, 175 species. There are seventeen varieties of oak alone. "There are many kinds of nut trees in Kentucky," says Miriam Moore, who grew up in southeastern Kentucky. "And anyone who knows where to look can have a snack just for the picking." She and her friends were given strict instructions to stay on the paths while exploring the woods, since the trees are so thick you can lose sight of the trail after just a few steps.

The smallest known flowering plant in the world lives in Kentucky. This plant, the watermeal, is no larger than a pinhead and produces microscopic flowers. Kentucky is also home to goldenrod, azaleas, buttercups, mountain laurel, and rhododendrons. In springtime, these flowering plants splash color across hills and meadows. The most famous plant in Kentucky, the one that gave the state its nickname, is not native to the Americas. Bluegrass was brought to the area by English settlers around 1625. It has spread over most of central Kentucky, and for much of the year looks like regular grass. But in the spring, its new blades turn the hills of central Kentucky a soft blue-green color.

More than three hundred species of birds grace Kentucky's skies. The largest and most spectacular are bald eagles, hawks, and ospreys. Shy wild turkeys roam the woods, and owls hunt there at night. They are joined by many mammals. The largest are black

Springtime brings dazzling wildflower displays.

bear and white tailed deer. Coyotes are occasionally seen, and skunks, mice, shrews, and river otters abound. Raccoons, squirrels, possums, and other small mammals thrive in the mild climate Naturally, with so much water, many fish live in Kentucky. You will find many a Kentuckian down by their favorite stream, casting for bass, walleye, sucker, crappie, rainbow trout, and sauger.

Kentucky's wildlife used to be even more diverse than it is today. Some of the earliest animals—mastodons, woolly mammoths, big-horned bison, giant armadillos, and giant sloths—became extinct

Wild turkeys are common in Kentucky's woods.

The white-tailed deer is one of the largest mammals living in Kentucky today.

as the climate changed. Later, early white settlers drove away such animals as elk, cougars, and wolves. In the eighteenth century, Kentucky had 18 million acres of forest, 2 million acres of prairie, and 1.6 million acres of wetlands. Today, the forests have shrunk to 13 million acres. No prairies remain, and the wetlands have shrunk to less than one-quarter their former size. Some of the animals that called the forests, prairies, and wetlands home have also disappeared.

A quiet stream is the perfect spot for fishing.

Some trees that were once common in Kentucky's forests are now scarce. Many of Kentucky's beautiful chestnut trees were destroyed in a blight that lasted much of the nineteenth century. The majestic elms that grew to towering heights were almost totally wiped out by Dutch elm disease, a parasite introduced to North America in 1916. Most of the state's huge, ancient oaks were felled for lumber. While oaks still grow in Kentucky, very few of them approach the height or girth of their ancestors. In fact, most trees in Kentucky's

Kudzu grows quickly and sometimes engulfs entire trees and even buildings.

forests today are smaller than those of a few centuries ago.

Recently, some trees in Kentucky have become covered by thick vines, which makes them look like giant green sock puppets or Muppets. The vines, called kudzu, gradually choke the life out of the trees. Their broad leaves keep the sunlight from reaching the tree. Kudzu is grown in Japan as food for both humans and cattle and was introduced into the American South as a decorative plant. But because it has no natural predators in Kentucky, it has grown out of control. People try to cut it down, but it grows so fast that many give up. "If you sit and watch it for a few minutes, you can actually see it grow," says frustrated farmer Kathy Simpson. "Since it grows where your cattle graze, you don't want to use a strong herbicide on it and poison the animals. I suppose I'll have to learn to live with it."

Kentucky's history is filled with stories of men and women surviving despite many difficult obstacles and hardships. This same perseverance and resourcefulness should help Kentuckians as they grapple with the challenges of protecting their state's lovely countryside.

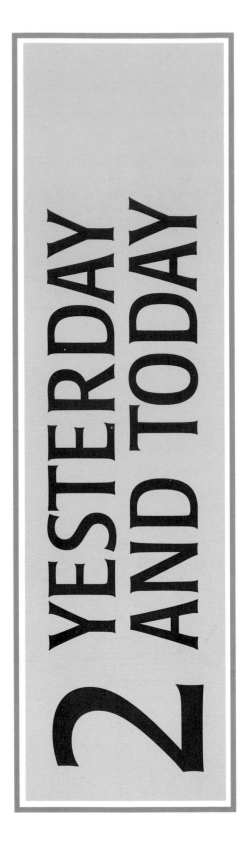

2 YESTERDAY AND TODAY

Cherokee Park Landscape, by Carl C. Brenner

The first humans to arrive in what is now Kentucky followed mastodons and other large animals into the area 12,000 years ago. These prehistoric people probably did not stay put in any one place.

THE FIRST KENTUCKIANS

About 10,000 years later, people of the Adena culture settled in north-central Kentucky. They established villages, mostly along rivers, and planted crops. They lived in houses made of wood and dried mud and buried their dead in huge mounds, some of which can still be seen. No one knows where the Adena Indians went; perhaps they moved on to another place, or maybe they stayed and merged with the next arrivals, the Hopewell culture. The Hopewell developed extensive trade networks with peoples as far away as present-day Michigan.

By the time whites arrived in the area in the seventeenth century, few Indians lived there. Only some small villages of Shawnees, descendants of people who had lived in eastern Kentucky, dotted the landscape. No one knows why this fertile and beautiful land was largely uninhabited.

Although few Indians lived in what is now Kentucky, the area

Shawnee villages were scattered throughout Kentucky when the first Europeans entered the region.

was used as a hunting ground by many tribes, including the Shawnees, Cherokees, Chickasaws, Wyandots, Delawares, and Iroquois. For the most part, these groups had few conflicts. But eventually that changed. During the seventeenth and eighteenth centuries, the Iroquois traded skins to Dutch colonists in return for guns and then chased out many of their rivals.

Some Shawnees resisted the Iroquois aggression and the later flood of white settlers. By canoe and foot, the Shawnees could reach

THE PLEIADES AND THE PINE: A CHEROKEE TALE

One day seven young boys were playing ball when they were supposed to be working. Their mothers scolded them, and they ran off into the woods to the spot where dances were held.

They started dancing around and around. They danced for so long that their mothers got worried and came to look for them. As their mothers drew near, they saw the boys dancing. But as they watched, the boys' feet began rising off the earth. The women ran to grab their sons, but it was too late—the boys were floating high above their reach. One mother made a great leap, seized her son's foot, and pulled him to the ground. But she had pulled too hard, and her son hit the ground with such force that he sunk into it and disappeared from sight.

The other six boys continued dancing and rising as their weeping mothers called to them. They finally ascended into the sky and became the constellation Ani'tsutsa (the Boys), which is commonly known as the Pleiades. The mother whose son had plunged into the earth came to cry over him every day, until a green plant grew up out of the soil where he lay. It eventually became the tall tree called the pine, which the Cherokees say is of the same nature as the stars.

the Great Lakes, the Atlantic Ocean, and the Gulf of Mexico. Game was plentiful. They had no intention of moving to a less comfortable place, and they struggled fiercely to keep their lands. They finally lost the fight in 1774, when colonial troops defeated them in a bloody battle to end Lord Dunmore's War. The Shawnees were forced to give up their hunting grounds south of the Ohio River.

THE FRONTIER PASSES BY

By this time, the abundant game and fertile land were attracting droves of European settlers. English explorers had first come through the area in the mid-1600s, and the Frenchman René-Robert Cavelier, Sieur de La Salle may have explored the region in his travels of 1669 to 1671. The Appalachian Mountains, however, were hard to cross, and only a few hunters and trappers followed.

Exploring Kentucky was difficult. Its woods are so thick that it is hard to take more than a few steps without brushing aside a branch, tripping over a root, or finding yourself hemmed in by shrubbery. Add to this the oppressive heat and humidity and the mountainous, rocky terrain, and many modern travelers would feel like giving up after a short walk. It is little wonder that when people left their homes in the East for the wilds of Kentucky, their families often held funerals for them.

Thomas Walker, a doctor from Virginia, aided exploration of the region immensely when he found a low spot in the mountains in 1750. The Cumberland Gap, as this pass was called, soon became the most important route to the west. The historian Frederick Jackson Turner once wrote, "Stand at Cumberland Gap and watch the procession of civilization, marching single file—the buffalo following the trail to the salt springs, the Indian, the fur-trader and hunter, the cattle-raiser, the pioneer farmer—and the frontier has passed by."

Fabled explorer Daniel Boone made his first trip through the Cumberland Gap in 1767, and in 1775 he helped blaze a trail through Kentucky's forests, the Wilderness Road. Boone's exploring

Daniel Boone first glimpsed Kentucky when he passed through the Cumberland Gap in 1767.

skills were legendary, and he himself once said that he had never gotten lost, exactly, but was "sometimes bewildered." His Wilderness Road became the major trail west for pioneers.

THE GROWTH OF A STATE

In 1774, James Harrod led a group of colonists through the gap and founded Harrodsburg, Kentucky's first permanent white settlement. A year later, Daniel Boone established a fort at a site he called Boonesborough.

After the American colonies declared their independence from Britain in 1776, the British encouraged Indians to attack whites in the newly settled areas of the Southeast. Boonesborough was one of the towns attacked. Early settlers often took refuge in Boone's fort during these attacks.

At the end of the American Revolution, Kentucky had a population of only about 12,000 and was still part of the state of Virginia. Between 1775 and 1795, more than 100,000 people poured through the Cumberland Gap. Some continued west, but many

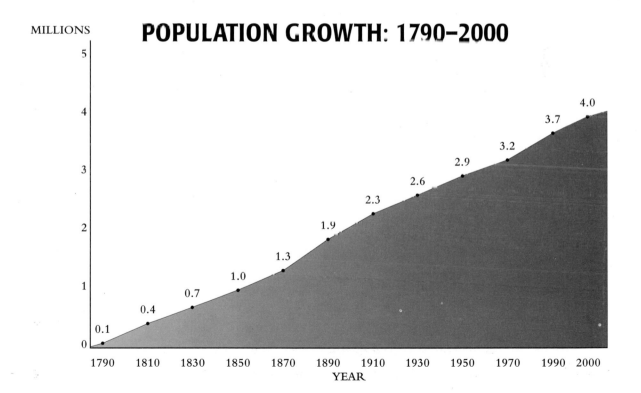

POPULATION GROWTH: 1790–2000

A LITTLE HERO

In 1791, a group of settlers traveling down the Ohio River was attacked by Indians. Three of the nine men in the party were killed and four were seriously wounded. One of the survivors wrote:

The women and children were all uninjured excepting a little son of Mr. Plascut, who after the battle was over, came to the Captain, and with great coolness, requested him to take a ball [bullet] out of his head. On examination it appeared that a ball that had passed through the side of the boat, had penetrated the forehead of this little hero and remained under the skin. The Captain took it out, when the lad observed, *"that is not all,"* raised his arm and exhibited a piece of bone at the point of his elbow, which had been shot off and hung by the skin. His mother exclaimed, "why did you not tell me of this?" "Because," he cooly replied, "the Captain directed us to be silent during the action, and I thought you would be likely to make a noise if I told you."

remained in Kentucky to take advantage of the fertile farmland and abundant hunting. By 1790, Kentucky's population had boomed to more than 70,000, and two years later Kentucky became the fifteenth state.

Because of the rich farmland, especially in the Bluegrass Region, agriculture quickly became the most important source of income in the state. After the steamboat was invented in the early nineteenth century, agricultural products could be more easily shipped to other parts of the country. Kentucky thrived, as its farmers sold huge quantities of hemp, corn, tobacco, wheat, and flax.

A STATE DIVIDED

Most crops were raised at least in part by slave labor. Black Americans had been in Kentucky as long as white settlers. An Indian attack in 1775 on Daniel Boone's party as it was carving out the Wilderness Road had killed at least one slave. Slaves never made up more than 24 percent of Kentucky's population. Although this number may seem large, in the Deep South, more than half the population were slaves. Most enslaved Kentuckians labored in fields, while some worked in mining and manufacturing.

Kentucky's farms were generally smaller than those in the other slave states. Most slaveholding farmers owned fewer than five slaves.

The invention of the steamship helped farmers get their crops to market.

THE HUNTERS OF KENTUCKY

Frontier bragging was very much an accepted form of expression. Andrew Jackson's Kentucky riflemen let it be known that they were "half horse–half alligator." This song details their exploits against the British at the Battle of New Orleans, January 8, 1815. It was later used as a campaign song for Jackson in the presidential election of 1824.

Ye gen-tle-men and la-dies fair who grace this fa-mous ci-ty, Just lis-ten, if you've time to spare, while I re-hearse a dit-ty; And for this op-por-tu-ni-ty con-ceive your-selves quite luck-y, For 'tis not of-ten that you see a hun-ter from Ken-tuck-y.

Chorus

O, Ken-tuck-y, the hun-ters of Ken-tuck-y.

We are a hardy, free-born race,
Each man to fear a stranger;
Whate'er the game we join in chase,
Despoiling time and danger;
And if a daring foe annoys,
Whate're his strength and forces,
We'll show him that Kentucky boys
Are alligator horses. *Chorus*

I s'pose you've read it in the prints,
How Packenham attempted
To make old Hickory Jackson wince,
But soon his scheme repented;
For we, with rifles ready cocked,
Thought such occasion lucky,
And soon around the gen'ral flocked
The hunters of Kentucky. *Chorus*

You've heard, I s'pose, how New Orleans
Is famed for wealth and beauty,
There's girls of ev'ry hue it seems,
From snowy white to sooty;
So Packenham he made his brags,
If he in fight was lucky,
He'd have their girls and cotton bags,
In spite of old Kentucky. *Chorus*

But Jackson, he was wide awake,
And was not scared of trifles;
For well he knew what aim we take
With our Kentucky rifles;

He led us down to Cypress Swamp,
The ground was low and mucky;
There stood John Bull in pomp,
And here was old Kentucky. *Chorus*

A bank was raised to hide our breasts,
Not that we thought of dying,
But that we always like to rest,
Unless the game is flying;
Behind it stood out a little force,
None wished it to be greater,
For every man was half a horse
And half an alligator. *Chorus*

They did not let our patience tire,
Before they showed their faces;
We did not choose to waste our fire,
So snugly kept our places;
But when so near we saw them wink,
We thought it time to stop 'em,
And 'twould have done you good, I think,
To see Kentuckians drop 'em. *Chorus*

They found, at last, 'twas vain to fight,
Where lead was all the booty,
And so they wisely took to flight,
And left us all our beauty;
And now, if danger e'er annoys,
Remember what our trade is,
Just send for us Kentucky boys,
And we'll protect ye, ladies. *Chorus*

A SLAVE AUCTION

Isaac Johnson's mother was a slave and his father was a slave owner. His father sold his family when he was eleven years old. He later wrote:

I was [sold] for seven hundred dollars . . . to William Madinglay, who came forward and said: "Come along with me, boy, you belong to me." I said to him: "Let me go and see my mother." He answered me crossly: "Come along with me, I will train you without your mother's help." I was taken to one side and chained to a post as though I had been a horse. . . .

The next to be set up was my mother. . . .

The next sale was of Eddie, my little brother, whom we all loved so much, he was sold for two hundred dollars. . . . Thus, in a very short time, our happy family was scattered, without even the privilege of saying "Good by" to each other, and never again to be seen, at least so far as I was concerned.

When a slaveholder sold his slaves, families were frequently split up.

In Kentucky, blacks, both slave and free, were treated quite differently from whites. There were four crimes for which a white person could be executed, while eleven crimes were considered severe enough to execute a black.

Most of the time, slaves had no choice but to put up with their miserable conditions. But in a few cases, slaves took matters into their own hands. In the most famous uprising in Kentucky, in August 1818, between fifty-five and seventy-five slaves armed themselves and tried to escape to freedom. They got into a gun battle with the state militia, and most were recaptured.

Black and white pupils studied together at Berea College.

But some white Kentuckians refused to accept the poor treatment of blacks. Before the Civil War, Berea College was founded with the aim of providing a college education to anyone who wanted one, whatever the student's race, religion, or ability to pay. From the time it opened, blacks and whites studied together. But in 1904, a state law declared it illegal for black and white students to attend classes together. Not until 1950 was Berea permitted to admit black students again.

Throughout the first half of the nineteenth century, the right of individual states to make their own laws, including deciding whether slavery would be legal, was hotly debated between North and South. Kentucky was torn. On one hand, it had passed a law in 1833 forbidding slaves to be brought into the state for resale. On the other hand, most Kentuckians had come from the Southern slaveholding states.

When these states seceded and formed the Confederate States of America, Kentucky decided to stay with the Union. But after the Civil War started, some people sympathetic to the Confederacy in western and central Kentucky formed their own government and were admitted into the Confederate States of America. Some 35,000 Kentuckians fought for the Confederacy, while about 70,000 fought for the Union. Both sides included a star to represent Kentucky in their flags. Not only the state, but towns and even families were divided. One former Kentucky governor had two sons. One was a general in the Confederate army, and the other a general in the Union army. Both Abraham Lincoln, president of the United States during the Civil War, and Jefferson Davis, president of the Confederate States of America, were born in Kentucky.

Early in the war, Kentuckian George R. Browder wrote in his diary, "I think we will have dark days in [Kentucky], & it will be long perhaps before the war is over." He was right.

No large Civil War battles took place in Kentucky. The Battle of Perryville, in October 1862, was the bloodiest, with 7,500 soldiers killed or wounded. But during the war the state was overrun by guerrillas fighting small skirmishes and raiding and burning down homes. Many farms were damaged or destroyed. Some Kentuckians, despairing of ever being able to make a living from agriculture again, turned to manufacturing. When the war ended in 1865, Kentucky found itself in desperate shape. Not only were its farms in ruins but the cities that had bought its produce had been devastated by the war and could no longer buy much.

Although civil rights were granted to Kentucky's blacks in 1865, relations between blacks and whites remained tense. In the fifteen years following the war, almost 150 blacks were executed by a mob, or lynched. Public education for Kentucky's blacks was established, but there was so little funding that very few actually attended school.

Although black Kentuckians won their freedom with the Civil War, most continued to endure dire poverty.

COAL AND TOBACCO

After the Civil War, the nation and the world became more dependent on manufacturing, increasing the demand for coal. Coal was also used to fuel the railroads, which were expanding rapidly at this time. Because Kentucky had a large coal supply, its economy began to revive from the horrors of the war.

The development of hardier strains of tobacco, which grew well in Kentucky, was also a boon to the state's economy. Tobacco production in Kentucky tripled between 1870 and 1900, and it became the state's most important crop.

Realizing how profitable tobacco was, some growers banded together to try to raise the price paid for tobacco in the region. Some farmers resisted joining these cooperatives. The result was several years of violence in the so-called Black Patch War, which was named for the dark leaves of one kind of tobacco. Between 1905 and 1909, night riders, who called themselves "Possum Hunters," terrorized the farmers who refused to band together. They burned farms, destroyed fields, and whipped and murdered their opponents. After years of violence, the conflict finally died down with neither side the winner.

In 1917, the United States entered World War I. By the war's end, 80,000 Kentuckians had served in the armed forces. In Breathitt County, not a single man had to be drafted because so many eligible men signed up voluntarily. This was the only county in the entire country where this happened.

World War I caused a huge increase in the need for coal, bringing prosperity to Kentucky. Many farmers sold their land and went to work in the mines. But when the war ended, so did the great

Disputes among tobacco growers brought guns into the field during the Black Patch War.

demand for coal. With no farms to return to, many Kentuckians went broke.

Those who still had jobs in the mines were hardly better off. Not only did they do dirty, dangerous work, but they were poorly paid. Most lived in towns built by the mining companies and bought their goods at high prices in stores the companies owned as well. The miners and the mine owners clashed frequently, and often violently. Harlan County, the scene of much of the fighting, was called "Bloody Harlan."

During the Great Depression of the 1930s, when the U.S. economy went into a tailspin, Kentucky suffered more than most states.

A series of wage cuts in the early 1930s left Kentucky coal miners with only three or four dollars each month for food. "It was time to fight," said one man involved in the strikes, "while we still could fight."

Farmers and miners had few reserves to fall back on, and when banks failed to make farm loans and coal mines closed down, the workers had few skills to transfer to new jobs. The government tried to help by constructing power plants and phone lines, which brought electricity and telephone service to much of the state for the first time. Roads and schools were also improved. Kentucky's economy didn't really rebound until the beginning of World War II, which again increased the demand for coal.

TO THE PRESENT

In the years after the war, some Kentuckians turned their attention to the injustices suffered by the state's black citizens. For decades,

The government created jobs for many Kentuckians who had been thrown out of work during the Great Depression. These men are building a sewer in Paducah.

blacks had been forced to attend separate schools from whites, and they endured widespread discrimination in all walks of life.

But gradually, legal discrimination began to be stripped away. In the mid-1950s, Louisville became the first large southern city to admit blacks to schools that had previously only allowed whites. Although some white Kentuckians resisted it, this integration of the public schools was more peaceful than it would be in the coming years in many other states. In 1964, civil rights leader Martin

Louisville citizens stage a sit-in to protest segregation.

Luther King Jr. led a march in Frankfort to encourage the passage of a civil rights law. Although this bill did not pass, two years later Kentucky became the first southern state to enact such a law.

Kentuckians have worked hard to make their state a good place to live. They have a proud tradition to draw on. Author Wendell Berry once wrote that in Kentucky forests you can feel the presence of "the ancient tribesmen who used to inhabit the rock houses of the cliffs; of the white hunters from east of the mountains; of the farmers who accepted the isolation of these nearly inaccessible valleys. . . . If one spends much time here and feels much liking for the place, it is hard to escape the sense of one's predecessors." Many Kentuckians would be quick to agree, as they strive to live up to their state's great heritage.

3 MAKING KENTUCKY WORK

The capitol in Frankfort

Pioneer Kentucky was a rough place. Until 1799, when the first prison was built, all serious crimes were punished by death, since there were no facilities for holding prisoners. A lot has changed since then. Today, Kentucky has an extensive court system, and this once-violent state has a crime control record to be proud of.

INSIDE GOVERNMENT

Like the United States, Kentucky has three branches of government: executive, legislative, and judicial.

Executive. Kentucky's governor proposes the state budget to the legislature and signs bills into law. But the governor has less power than in some states. For example, if the governor vetoes (refuses to sign) a bill, the legislature can vote on it again. If a majority is still in favor of the bill, the governor's veto is overridden, and the bill becomes law anyway. In most states, it takes a two-thirds vote to override a veto. Also, Kentucky's governor cannot serve two terms in a row.

Martha Layne Collins became Kentucky's first woman governor in 1983. She had first entered the public eye as Queen of the Kentucky Derby Festival. She was a junior high school teacher until she became involved in Democratic Party politics. As governor, she

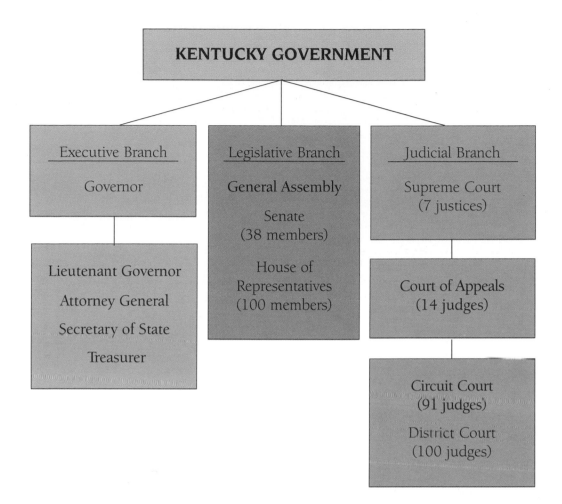

KENTUCKY GOVERNMENT

Executive Branch
Governor

Lieutenant Governor
Attorney General
Secretary of State
Treasurer

Legislative Branch
General Assembly

Senate
(38 members)

House of
Representatives
(100 members)

Judicial Branch
Supreme Court
(7 justices)

Court of Appeals
(14 judges)

Circuit Court
(91 judges)

District Court
(100 judges)

earned applause for reforming education and attracting new business to the state.

Legislative. The legislative branch is responsible for making the state laws. Kentucky's legislature, called the General Assembly, is made up of a senate, with thirty-eight members, and a house of representatives, with one hundred members. Senators serve four-year terms, and representatives serve two-year terms.

Judicial. Most trials in Kentucky start out in circuit courts, for serious offenses, or district courts, for less serious offenses. If some-

BLOODY POLITICS

These days, Kentucky politics is relatively peaceful, but it hasn't always been that way. Running for public office in the Bluegrass State used to be a hazardous business. A Democratic lawyer named William Goebel ran for governor in 1899. After a fierce campaign, Goebel appeared to have lost a close race to the Republican candidate, William S. Taylor. Although Goebel protested and an investigation of the election began, Taylor was sworn in as governor. But then Goebel was shot on the steps of the state capitol. The next day, the legislature, which was controlled by Democrats, declared that Goebel had actually won the election. Before Goebel died three days later, the Democrats swore him into office.

Some Democrats insisted that the Republicans had been behind Goebel's assassination. Taylor fled to Indiana, and his secretary of state and two other men were convicted of the murder. Questions about what really happened persist to this day.

William Goebel

one is dissatisfied with a verdict in a circuit or district court, he or she can ask a court of appeals to look at their case. The appeals court judges decide whether the original trial was fair.

The highest court in Kentucky is the supreme court, which has seven justices, one from each region of the state. The supreme court decides whether rulings made by the lower courts are in line with the state constitution. It also reviews all trials that involve the death penalty or a prison sentence of more than twenty years. Supreme court justices are elected for eight-year terms, starting in different years, which prevents any group of judges from getting too much power.

MAKING THE GRADE

Kentuckians saw the importance of education from the beginning. Kentucky's Transylvania University, founded in 1780, was the first college west of the Allegheny Mountains.

Although Kentucky established public schools in 1849, the state was not wealthy and could not put much money into them. For more than a hundred years, education in Kentucky was worse than in most of the country. Miriam Moore, who attended public schools in rural Kentucky in the 1940s, recalls that many parents bitterly resented the government forcing their children to attend school when the parents needed them to work in the fields. "Although the law said that they had to go, the officials kind of closed their eyes when parents kept their children at home. Once in a while, the driver of the school bus would shout, 'Everybody down!' and we'd all have to lie on the floor. I didn't know it then, but what the bus driver was afraid of was someone shooting at him through the windows and hitting the kids." Moore says she was lucky to have a bus to ride in. Two boys nearby had to travel on a mule. Her school had no running water, and when a student had to visit the outhouse, the teacher would come along, carrying a gun. In this case the worry was not angry parents, but the wild boars that roamed the woods.

Becky Ray grew up in central Kentucky in the 1950s and 1960s. She saw firsthand how difficult it was to get an education in the country. "Even though our school was only ten miles away, it took us an hour and a half to get there on the bus," she says, "because there were so many kids living far apart for the bus driver to stop for." When Ray's family moved to the city, she quickly realized how sorely lacking her education had been. "We moved to Louisville when I was in high school," she recalls, "and the kids were complaining about having to write a paper. I was terrified—no one had ever even asked me to write a book report."

Finally in 1988, sixty-four rural school districts sued the state government, saying that Kentucky had not lived up to its own constitution, which requires the state to have an efficient system of public schools. They argued that the rural schools were being neglected while those in the city were receiving more than their fair share of money. The entire school system was declared unconstitutional, and the Education Reform Act was passed in 1990 to improve the public schools. One of the act's most exciting innovations was to link smaller schools to larger ones by computer, so that a student in a small school can participate in classes in a city school hundreds of miles away. Improvements in education have been

In recent years, Kentucky has gone from having one of the worst school systems in the nation to having one of the best. Here, sixth graders do experiments on Earth Day.

dramatic. In 1996, the National Education Association named Kentucky's schools in the top three of all fifty states.

KENTUCKY AT WORK

Kentucky has long depended on coal mining for its livelihood. But this has been a mixed blessing. Although the industry provides a great deal of employment, coal mining is not pleasant work. One

EARNING A LIVING

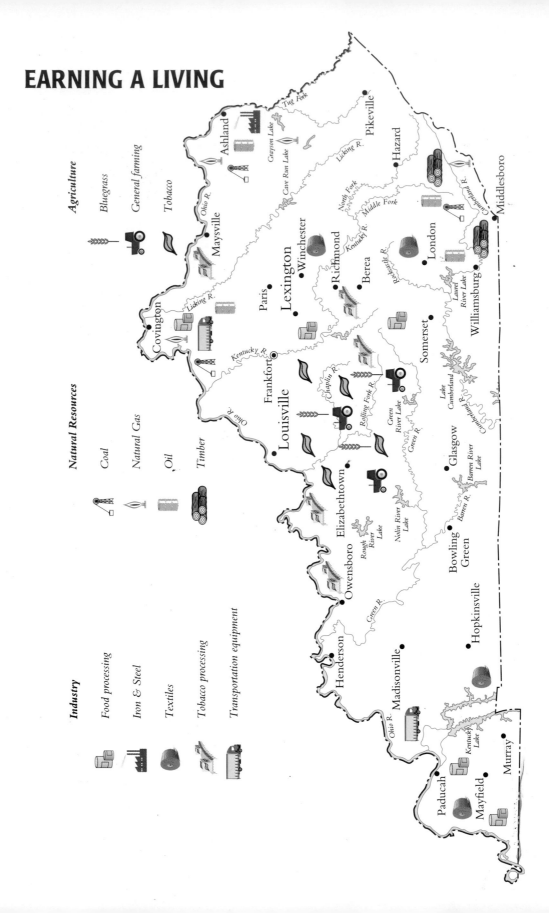

Agriculture

Bluegrass

General farming

Tobacco

Natural Resources

Coal

Natural Gas

Oil

Timber

Industry

Food processing

Iron & Steel

Textiles

Tobacco processing

Transportation equipment

Barges loaded with coal head up the Ohio River.

miner said, "It's the worst job in the world. It's the dirtiest. It's the most unhealthy and the most dangerous. . . . It's always muddy and nasty and you wade in it and you lay down in it and you can't stand up till you come back out. It's just miserable." But with the dismal state of education in Kentucky, until recently, many workers were not qualified for other jobs.

Coal mining also harms Kentucky itself. It causes erosion, destroys forests, and pollutes the water. Since 1977, mining companies have been legally obligated to restore the land they damage, and many do. Unfortunately, some companies manage to dodge the law, leaving vast areas of ruined land behind them.

Another problem with Kentucky's dependence on coal is that sometimes the demand for coal is low. When less coal is bought, coal companies close, and miners are out of work. This happened in the 1960s, and many Kentuckians left the state in search of other jobs. Then in the 1970s, a worldwide shortage of oil made people turn back to coal as a source of energy. Kentuckians poured back into the state in what has been called "the greatest reverse migration in history." In 1994, Kentucky tied with West Virginia for second place in coal production of all the fifty states, after Wyoming.

Agriculture is also important to Kentucky. The state's most valuable crop is tobacco. Kentucky produces more burley tobacco, a light-colored plant highly prized by cigarette manufacturers, than any other state. Kentuckians not only work in tobacco fields but they also support this industry by their habits. In 1996, a higher percentage of Kentuckians smoked tobacco than the residents of any other state.

Corn is another crop that has long been grown in Kentucky. Historically most Kentucky corn was sold as animal feed, but the state's farmers sometimes grew so much that they couldn't sell it all. A few began making whiskey from the leftover grain, and Kentucky's bourbon industry was born. Some of the bourbon makers operated illegally and refused to pay alcohol taxes to

TOBACCO

Tobacco has a long history in Kentucky. Tobacco pipes four to five thousand years old have been found in the state. The plant was prized by many Indian cultures. Some Native Americans used it in religious rituals or as medicine.

By the late 1700s, the tobacco industry was established among Kentucky's white settlers. Loüisville had factories that made cigars, pipe mixtures, snuff, and chewing tobacco.

Today, the future of tobacco in the state is uncertain. Because tobacco is dangerous to people's health, some politicians are trying to limit the amount of tobacco grown. They also want to make cigarettes more expensive so people will not buy as many. Some farmers are turning to other crops so they won't be so dependent on tobacco for their income. Others worry that the increasing restrictions will ruin their livelihood. "I don't smoke myself," says sixty-year-old tobacco farmer Jim Thornton, "but my family has owned this farm for four generations. I want my kids to inherit it, but it looks like they won't be able to. It's not good for growing anything but tobacco."

the government. Since they often worked at night by the light of the moon to avoid detection, they became known as "moonshiners," and their liquor was called "moonshine." A few people still make moonshine, but it is not nearly as common as it was in the early 1900s. Kentucky's legal alcohol, especially its famous bourbon, remains an important industry in the state today.

Livestock also brings a lot of money into Kentucky. The state's 250 horse farms, where some of the world's greatest racehorses are born, raised, and trained, provide work for thousands of Kentuckians and draw a lot of tourists. Less visible but equally important to the economy is the beef cattle industry.

BUILDING THE FUTURE

Kentucky has long been one of the nation's poorest states. It ranks near the bottom in terms of personal income. Likewise, its poverty

GROSS STATE PRODUCT: $96 BILLION

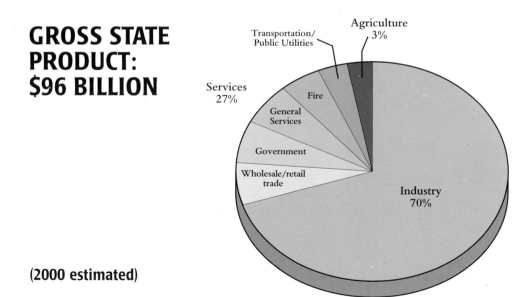

Transportation/Public Utilities

Agriculture 3%

Services 27%

Fire

General Services

Government

Wholesale/retail trade

Industry 70%

(2000 estimated)

Manufacturing has become increasingly important to Kentucky's economy.

rate is higher than the national average. But Kentucky is working hard to change this. Since the 1960s, the state has attracted more and more manufacturing. Motor vehicles, railroad cars, chemicals, clothing, elevators, typewriters, and steel are all made in Kentucky. The state has also been trying to help its economy by attracting more visitors. The amount of money brought in by tourists more than tripled during the 1990s. Today, about one-quarter of Kentucky's workers are in service jobs, which includes tourism.

Kentuckians have worked hard to improve the quality of life in their state, and their efforts show. Twelve-year-old Louisville native Jim Anderson says, "People should come here and see how great it is. They'd never want to leave."

4 PROUD PEOPLE

Almost all Kentuckians were born in the United States, and most of them were born in Kentucky. With their lovely countryside, thriving cities, and fascinating past, why would they live anywhere else? Kentuckians prove their love for their state by living out their lives where they were born.

A RURAL PAST

Kentuckians have always been drawn to the state's beautiful countryside. But the steep hills and narrow valleys made road construction difficult, so Kentuckians who didn't live in major cities were quite isolated. As recently as the 1960s, most Kentuckians lived in the country rather than in cities and towns. Even today, only about half the state's population is found in cities. Nationally, the proportion of city dwellers is closer to three-quarters.

Although Kentucky has grown more urban and prosperous in recent years, Kentuckians honor their diligent forebears who had to scrape a living off the land in such events as the International Bar-B-Q Festival, in Owensboro. The meat barbecued at this event is mutton—the meat from sheep—because sheep could thrive on even the state's most rugged, rocky terrain, which has only sparse vegetation, and cattle could not. Aside from barbecue tastings and

KENTUCKY HOT BROWN

This dish, named for Louisville's Brown Hotel, where it was first made, is a lunchtime favorite. Have an adult help you with this recipe.

2 tbsp. butter
2 tbsp. flour
1 cup hot milk
Salt and pepper
½ cup grated cheddar or American cheese
½ tsp. Worcestershire sauce
1 lb. sliced turkey breast
4 slices white toast
2 tbsp. grated Parmesan
8 slices bacon
8 strips canned pimento

Melt the butter. Add the flour and stir for one minute over low heat. Pour in the hot milk and whisk until smooth and thickened. Add salt and pepper to taste. Remove from heat, add the cheddar or American cheese and the Worcestershire sauce.

Meanwhile, grill the bacon in a pan.

On each slice of toast, arrange ¼ lb. turkey breast. Spread the sauce over it. Top with grated Parmesan, and crisscrosses of bacon and pimento. Broil until bubbling. Enjoy.

cook-offs, festival visitors are treated to a crafts fair, a fiddling contest, dancing, and a pie-eating contest.

Owensboro, the largest city in western Kentucky, also boasts its own regional stew, called burgoo. Each cook prepares burgoo in a different way, but all agree that it has to have a lot of ingredients, since the dish was originally made with the contributions of many people, each adding something different to the pot. Traditionalists insist that burgoo must include squirrel meat, but nowadays you're more likely to find cooks using mutton or beef.

LIVING TOGETHER

Only 20 percent of Kentuckians were born in a different state, one of the lowest proportions in the country. Less than 1 percent were

ETHNIC KENTUCKY

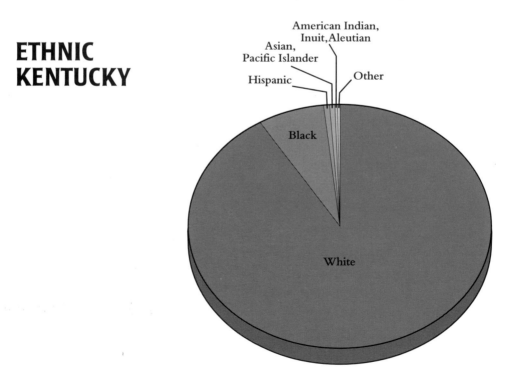

Mexican immigrants working on a tobacco farm

born in a different country. This often makes Kentuckians wary of strangers. After three years in rural southeastern Kentucky, Miriam Moore says, "I made several good friends among the children. But the parents were always hostile, and they were relieved to see the strangers go after three to four years."

Most Kentuckians are of European descent, primarily English, German, Irish, and Scottish. Blacks make up about 7 percent of the population while Asians and Native Americans each comprise less than 1 percent.

Race relations in the state have long been troubled, but many think the situation is improving. Mary Anderson, a white woman who has lived in Kentucky all of her seventy-nine years, says, "Races are being accepted now more than they used to be. Integration may be slow, but it's coming. Many other races—not just blacks—are coming in: Hispanics, Arabs, Haitians. They are coming in from troubled spots all over the world."

Joyce Friend, an African American, agrees, but with some reservations. "I feel fine in the cities," she says, "but when I go to the country I sometimes feel that the white people wish I would stay away. I get waited on more slowly in stores than a white woman, and I often feel invisible. It's a relief to go back home to town."

RELIGION

Most Kentuckians identify themselves as Protestants, with Baptists accounting for nearly half of the total church membership. Baptists have been in Kentucky for more than two centuries, and many of them belong to small sects with names like Old Regular Baptists, Primitive Baptists, and Free Will Baptists. Some of these groups are very conservative in their beliefs and practices.

Kentuckians have long been known for their independence, and this is certainly true regarding religion. In some cases, a branch of religion will be represented by only one church with a tiny congregation.

One of the most interesting religious groups that made a home in Kentucky was the Society of Believers, who are often called the Shakers because of the rhythmic dances that formed part of their services. Shakers believed in living simply, worshiping God through work, and striving always to be perfect. In Kentucky, the Shakers had two main settlements: Pleasant Hill near Harrodsburg and South Union near Bowling Green. In the 1850s, there were about five thousand Shakers in the United States. But since their religion forbade them to marry and have children, the only way for the sect to grow was by recruiting new members. There are very few Shakers left today.

Baptists are the largest religious group in Kentucky.

"THE DARK AND BLOODY GROUND"

Until recently, Kentucky was known as one of the most violent areas of the United States. There are many possible reasons for this. Many Kentuckians lived in isolated communities, far from the law, and had to make their own justice. Sometimes this meant that the most powerful person or family in a hamlet ruled the town and decided what punishment was appropriate for what crime. Also, Kentuckians had a high rate of alcohol use, which often led to violent fights. Many carried weapons, so minor quarrels sometimes escalated into gunfights. In the nineteenth century, differences of opinion over whether Kentucky should go with the Union or the Confederacy led to tension between families and towns.

Many people think of feuds when Kentucky is mentioned. A feud is a violent quarrel that goes on for years or even generations. It often starts when a member of one group injures a person from another group, and someone from the injured person's side gets revenge. Then the first side avenges that injury, and so on, for years and years. From the mid-nineteenth to the early twentieth century, Kentucky's feuding families received much attention from newspapers. The press usually ignored the real reasons for the disagreements, which often originated in local economic or political struggles, and made it sound as though the "hillbillies" just enjoyed shooting each other for no reason.

The feuds did not end in the nineteenth century. Miriam Moore says that during her childhood before city dwellers went to the top of the ridge behind her town, where the more traditional country people lived, they would check with the storekeeper to see if it was

THE HATFIELDS AND THE McCOYS

Although not the nation's bloodiest feud, the conflict between the Kentucky McCoys and the West Virginia Hatfields is the best known. Until the 1860s, the two families lived in harmony. But then things changed, probably when a dead Union soldier from the McCoy family was found near the home of the pro-Confederacy Hatfields. The McCoys killed a Hatfield in revenge, and the feud took off.

In 1882, a Hatfield was murdered by three McCoys. The McCoys were caught, tied to a bush, and told by their Hatfield captors, "Boys, if you have any peace to make with your Maker you had better make it." Then, in the dim light of a lantern, they were shot.

The leader of the Hatfield clan, Devil Anse Hatfield, once said, "If you like you can say it is the devil's Church that I belong to." The McCoy leader, Randolph McCoy, said that no neighbor of the Hatfields could doubt the existence of the devil.

By the time the feud dwindled in the 1920s, somewhere between twelve and sixty-five people had been killed.

safe. "If someone was feuding, he'd tell them to keep out," she says. Although feuding has died down, it is still not limited to Kentucky's past.

KENTUCKY AT PLAY

People interested in old English, Scottish, and Irish customs love to visit Kentucky. "People are crazy about the Scottish games here," says Mary Jacobs, a Kentuckian of Scottish descent. "When the men dress

Scottish festivals are popular in Kentucky, which is home to many people of Scottish descent.

up in kilts and the bagpipes start to play, you could imagine you were in cold, gray Scotland instead of hot, sunny Kentucky!"

When people arrived from the British Isles in the eighteenth and nineteenth centuries, they brought their folk songs, dances, musical instruments, and stories with them. While many of these entertainments have changed or disappeared in Europe, in the hills of Kentucky they are still alive, and in many ways have changed little in the last century or two.

Set dancing, a form of folk dance that died out in Europe at the end of the nineteenth century, is still popular in Kentucky. Some dances are from the sixteenth century, while others probably go back to the Middle Ages.

These dances are sometimes accompanied by the dulcimer, a stringed instrument native to Appalachia but descended from the northern European zither. Another important instrument in Kentucky that developed in the Americas is the banjo, which is probably a combination of various ancestors, including an African gourd instrument and the mandolin.

The combination of British, country, folk, and slave songs led to the creation of an all-American form of music in Kentucky, named for the state's most famous characteristic. Bluegrass music is known throughout the world for its haunting melodies, beautiful lyrics, and often tragic love stories. Bill Monroe and the Blue Grass Boys were the first to popularize this traditional music, which uses the banjo, mandolin, fiddle, and other instruments. The headquarters of the International Bluegrass Music Association is in Owensboro, Kentucky.

Still another entertainment imported from Great Britain is

The mandolin is one of the mainstays of bluegrass music.

foxhunting. At the state's major foxhunts, visitors love to watch the beautiful horses, packs of dogs, and riders dressed in bright colors. At these events, foxes are not killed, just chased. The fox-hunt is mainly a chance for friends to ride their horses in the country and enjoy a traditional sport.

MAN O' WAR

Even people who know almost nothing about horses have heard of Man o' War. This chestnut thoroughbred was born near Lexington in 1917. He was considered unbeatable, and in fact he lost only one race in his career. Once he won by an unbelievable 100 times the length of a horse. As he won more and more races, his jockey was forced to carry handicap weights, intended to give the other horses a chance. They kept adding more and more weight until, in addition to the jockey, Man o' War was carrying 130 pounds in handicap weight.

His owner was once offered a million dollars for Man o' War, but he refused, saying "lots of men might have a million dollars, but only one man could have Man o' War." This magnificent horse was so popular that when he died in 1947, more than a thousand people attended his funeral.

Kentucky's real claim to fame is horse racing. The most famous horse race in the United States, the Kentucky Derby, has been run at Louisville's Churchill Downs every May since 1875. Thousands of people watch the world's best three-year-old thoroughbreds pound around the track each year. Man o' War, often called the greatest racehorse that ever lived, is buried in the center of the track (although, oddly enough, he never raced in the Kentucky Derby).

But the Kentucky Derby isn't just a horse race. The whole city celebrates for two weeks before the race with the Kentucky Derby Festival. One million people attend this citywide party, enjoying the world's largest annual fireworks show, concerts, and of course,

"All my friends go home for Derby," says one Louisville native who now lives in the Northeast. "It's when everyone gets together." The Pegasus Parade is a highlight of the Kentucky Derby (opposite).

many horse shows and exhibitions. "I love the Pegasus Parade that goes along with the Derby Festival," says Kentucky native Mary Anderson. "The horses are just beautiful. There is also a steamboat race, and a balloon race."

Working or playing, Kentuckians have their own unique style. Twelve-year-old Jim Anderson says, "Kentucky is not what people think it is. It is a busy state." The Kentuckians who take pride in their state and their heritage have made it that way.

5 DYNAMIC KENTUCKIANS

Men making wood tools

Exploration, politics, invention, music, sports, literature—Kentuckians have made contributions in so many areas that it would be impossible to list them all. Here are some of the most intriguing Kentuckians.

PUBLIC SERVICE

Esteemed politician Henry Clay was known as the Great Compromiser for his skill in getting opponents to agree with each other. He started his political career in the Kentucky legislature in 1803, when he was just twenty-six years old. He later served in the U.S. Senate, as the Speaker of the House of Representatives, and as secretary of state. Henry Clay is perhaps best remembered for his efforts to avoid the Civil War. He encouraged both North and South to accept some compromises that probably delayed the war. Although he lost all three of his campaigns for the presidency, Clay never abandoned his principles, saying, "I would rather be right than be president."

The twelfth president of the United States, Zachary Taylor, was born in Virginia. His family moved to Kentucky when he was only a few months old. Taylor grew up near Louisville, fought in the War of 1812, and was a hero in the Mexican War of the 1840s. His bravery earned him the nickname Old Rough and Ready. His "rough and

Henry Clay's efforts to prevent the Civil War earned him the nickname the Great Compromiser.

ready" reputation didn't please everyone, however, including his political opponent Daniel Webster, who called him "that swearing, whiskey drinking fighting frontier colonel." Later, Webster grew to admire the president's decisive nature, saying, "I don't often agree with the man, but he does make decisions." Zachary Taylor fell sick early in his presidency and died in 1850, having served only a little more than one year in office.

Jefferson Davis, the first and only president of the Confederate States of America, was born near Elkton, Kentucky, the youngest of ten children. He attended West Point and, like Zachary Taylor, was a hero of the Mexican War. He had a distinguished political career, serving in the U.S. Senate and as secretary of war. In 1844 a fellow politician described him as "the greatest man for soft words and hard arguments ever listened to."

Davis's growing unhappiness with what he saw as the federal government's interference in individual states' affairs caused him to switch loyalties to the Confederacy, the group of states that seceded from the Union. In 1861, Davis became the president of the Confederate States of America. When the Confederacy lost the Civil War, Davis was captured by Union forces, and he spent two

A man who knew Jefferson Davis said he "was a regular bulldog when he formed an opinion, for he would never let go."

Supreme Court justice Louis Brandeis was a staunch defender of free speech.

years in prison. After he was released, he traveled and eventually settled in Mississippi, where he spent the rest of his life.

Louis Brandeis, the first Jewish Supreme Court justice, was born in Louisville in 1856. He graduated from Harvard Law School at the tender age of twenty-two with the best grades in the school's history. He spent much of his legal career trying to help working people, fighting for low-cost life insurance, shorter workdays, and minimum-wage laws. He joined the Supreme Court in 1916 and continued working for social reform and human rights.

Kentucky's Young family has produced many remarkable civil rights advocates. Whitney Moore Young Sr. was once the head of the

Whitney Young Jr., who came from a prominent Kentucky family, was the head of the National Urban League. Here, he is meeting with President Lyndon Johnson.

department of engineering at the then all-black Lincoln Institute. He was later promoted to dean and to education director for the school. He was twice president of Kentucky's Negro Education Association and in 1964 was appointed by President Lyndon Johnson to oversee the implementation of civil rights laws. His son Whitney Moore Young Jr. was head of the National Urban League from 1961 until his death in 1971. He was a nationally recognized leader of the civil rights movement and helped open up many jobs and educational opportunities to African Americans. His sister Anita Young was one of the first African-American deans at the University of Louisville.

MUSIC

Not many people know that the most-sung tune in the world was written by two sisters from Louisville, Kentucky. Mildred and Patty Hill wrote "Good Morning to You," the tune used for "Happy Birthday to You," in 1893. But it is a very different kind of music that has made Kentucky famous: country and bluegrass. Kentucky has given the world such superstars as Red Foley, Billy Ray Cyrus, Crystal Gayle, Dwight Yoakam, and Patty Loveless.

Bill Monroe, the Father of Bluegrass Music, was born near

Bill Monroe once said, "If a man listening will let it, bluegrass will transmit right into your heart."

Rosine, Kentucky, and started playing the mandolin as a little boy. With his band, the Blue Grass Boys, he combined traditional mountain music with blues and gospel to form a new kind of music that eventually was called "bluegrass" after his group. When he debuted on the Grand Ole Opry, country music's most famous radio show, in 1939, the audience went wild after his first song, "Mule Skinner Blues." There was so much applause that he and his band had to do an encore—the first time this had happened in the program's ten-year history. Monroe was inducted into the Country Music Hall of Fame in 1970.

Loretta Lynn was the first woman ever to win the Country Music Association's Entertainer of the Year Award. Her autobiography, *Coal Miner's Daughter*, told about her life in Butcher Hollow, Kentucky, where she lived in poverty with her large and loving family. Loretta Lynn married at age thirteen and by age eighteen was the mother of four children. She often played guitar to her children and sang them lullabies. With her husband's encouragement, she started singing in restaurants and bars, which launched her career in country music. In 1980, *Coal Miner's Daughter* was made into a movie that brought country music to the attention of many Americans who until then had not listened to it.

Jean Ritchie also came from a large and loving family. The Ritchie family was so well known for singing traditional mountain songs that folk music collectors would often visit to hear them perform the old tunes. Many of these songs were traditional English ballads that Jean's great-grandfather had brought with him when he immigrated to America. Other songs her family had learned from neighbors. "Because we Ritchies loved to sing so well," she once

Jean Ritchie plays the dulcimer, a traditional Appalachian instrument. "I used to tell people how easy it is to play and they wouldn't believe me," she says.

said, "we always listened to people singing songs we didn't know, and we caught many good ones that way." Jean, the youngest of fourteen children, started playing the dulcimer at age five. She grew up to be a teacher and a social worker, incorporating music wherever she could in her work. She eventually turned all her attention to her true love and became a folk singer. In her long career, she has made almost forty albums and has introduced American folk music to audiences the world over.

The mother-daughter singers Naomi and Wynonna Judd, who were both born in Ashland, Kentucky, always knew they had special talent. But like many people who want to be musicians, they had a hard time getting anybody to listen to them. Naomi was a nurse in Tennessee when they got their lucky break. The father of one of her patients worked in the record industry and arranged for them to have an audition with RCA records in 1983. Almost immediately, their sweet but strong voices and distinctive song styling made them stars. In addition to five Grammys, the Judds have won eight Country Music Association awards.

Naomi and Wynonna Judd are among country music's most popular performers.

William Wells Brown was one of the first African Americans to publish a novel.

LITERATURE

Something about Kentucky seems to inspire great writers. The state has turned out a host of novelists, poets, humorists, and essayists, many of whom write about their love for Kentucky.

William Wells Brown was born into slavery near Lexington. He escaped to freedom in 1834. Later, while working on a ferryboat on Lake Erie, he helped sixty-nine slaves escape. His first book, an autobiography entitled *Narrative of William Wells Brown, a Fugitive Slave, Written by Himself*, was published in 1847. In this and other works, he wrote about the experience of slavery and about African-American soldiers in the Civil War. Before he died in 1884, he had become among the first African Americans to publish a novel, a play, and a travel book.

Esteemed writer Robert Penn Warren was born in Guthrie, Kentucky, in 1905. Although he originally intended to be a chemist, Warren discovered his love for writing during college. His most famous book, *All the King's Men*, about the career of an

Robert Penn Warren was one of the most highly acclaimed writers to emerge from Kentucky.

"THESE HILLS I LOVE"

In this poem, Jesse Stuart shows his deep love for his home state.

THESE HILLS I LOVE

This night a million stars pin back the sky
To make a jeweled roof above this earth
And I must go to hear the night winds cry
Over these ancient hills that gave me birth.
I will hear messages from whispering leaves
That grow from trees in forests such as mine
Where beech and birch and ash are friendly trees,
Where sycamore is neighbor to the pine.
For months I've been away from life my own,
I've heard the song of wheels against cold steel;
I've climbed skyward, trusting the motors' moan
Across the continent. And, now, I feel
The sweet true surge of life in every vein,
Herein this night with brighter stars above
With beauty, song and peace to soothe my brain
Among these rugged hills of home I love.

unscrupulous southern politician, was made into a popular movie. Over the course of his long career, Warren won many awards, including three Pulitzer Prizes. He was also named the first poet laureate (official poet) of the United States.

Jesse Hilton Stuart has often written about his beloved home state. He was born in northeast Kentucky into a family of tenant farmers. As a child, Stuart resolved that one day he would buy all the farms where his parents had worked. Through his parents he learned to love Kentucky's hill country and to appreciate education, even though his father never learned to read or write and his mother had completed only second grade. All five Stuart children graduated from college. Stuart worked as a teacher, a school principal, and a school superintendent before turning to writing. He wrote many books, including a collection of poetry entitled *Kentucky is My Land*. He was named poet laureate of Kentucky in 1954. In 1980 he fulfilled his childhood dream: he finished buying all seven hundred acres of farmland that his parents had worked and donated it to the state as a nature preserve.

SPORTS

Kentuckians love sports, although the state has no major-league teams. Basketball is particularly popular. This is partly due to the efforts of Adolph Rupp, the head basketball coach at the University of Kentucky from 1930 to 1972. Under his leadership, Kentucky won an incredible 876 games, giving Rupp the most wins of any college basketball coach at that time, a record he held for twenty-five years. During his astonishingly long and successful career, Kentucky won four national championships and twenty-seven Southeastern Conference championships.

The great boxer Muhammad Ali was born Cassius Clay in Louisville. As a young man, he started boxing to earn money and quickly showed amazing talent. He won many titles as an amateur, including a gold medal at the 1960 Olympics. Clay's charm and personality attracted the attention of many people who had never been interested in boxing before. He became the Heavyweight

Adolph Rupp's teams won 876 games during his forty-two years as head coach of the University of Kentucky basketball team.

Boxing Champion of the World in 1964, the same year that he converted to Islam and changed his name to Muhammad Ali. As a Muslim, he refused to serve in the Vietnam War, and he was fined and sentenced to five years in prison. Ali never went to prison, but he lost his championship title and was barred from the boxing ring for three years. During his absence from boxing, he became a passionate spokesperson for civil rights.

As soon as the ban was lifted, Ali returned to the ring. He

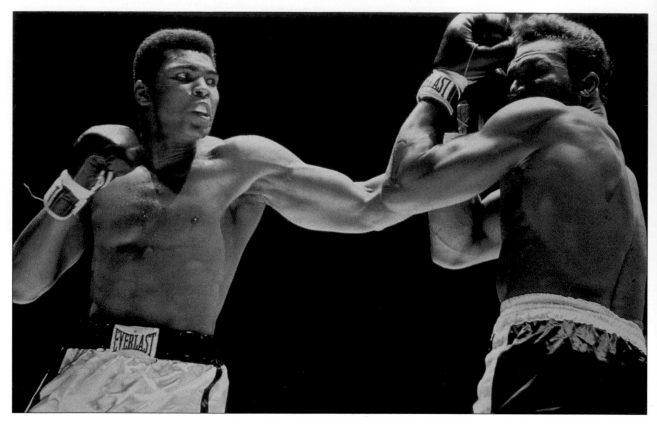

During his phenomenal career, Muhammad Ali earned more money than every previous heavyweight boxing champion combined.

defeated George Forman in 1974 to regain his heavyweight title. Ali retired from boxing in 1981. Tragically, the many blows to his head caused him to develop Parkinson's syndrome, and he now has difficulty speaking.

ON YOUR TABLE

Some of the most popular foods in the United States originated in Kentucky. America's best-selling fast food is fried chicken, and the king of fried chicken is KFC, formerly called Kentucky Fried Chicken. This company was founded in Kentucky by Colonel Harland Sanders. Colonel Sanders owned Sanders' Cafe in Corbin, Kentucky, where his fried chicken recipe was so popular that he decided to concentrate on that one dish alone. He founded Kentucky Fried Chicken in 1956, and the rest is history. In Louisville, the Colonel Harland Sanders Museum explains how he made it big.

Although you have probably not heard of Louisville pharmacist John Colgan, you are surely aware of his invention: chewing gum. Before Colgan came along, the only product people had for chewing was tree sap. Originally called Colgan's Taffy Tolu, the chewing gum was introduced in 1893 and was an instant hit, not only in the United States, but around the world.

6 A BLUEGRASS TOUR

No matter what kind of scenery you're looking for, Kentucky has it—except desert and seashore, that is. Beautiful mountains, rolling hills, fertile farmland, lakes, rivers, caves—you'll find it all in the Bluegrass State. Nearly 70 percent of the United States population can reach Kentucky in one day's drive, and many tourists take advantage of this easy access. Kentucky has encouraged tourism, building parks and attractions that are fun for everyone to see. Their efforts have paid off. Today, tourism is thriving in Kentucky.

THE MOUNTAINOUS EAST

Most visitors to eastern Kentucky are drawn by natural wonders: the Appalachian Mountains, the caves, the rivers, the beautiful parks. But don't leave eastern Kentucky without exploring the exciting cities and towns, too.

Historic Ashland is a great place to see centuries of Kentucky history all in one place. The families who began settling there in the eighteenth century built houses in the midst of ancient Indian burial mounds from two thousand years earlier. Today, visitors can tour the mounds as well as many ornate eighteenth- and nineteenth-century homes. One even has two cast-iron dragons glaring down from its roof. Based in a 1917 mansion, the Kentucky Highlands Museum teaches visitors about the region's past, with

PLACES TO SEE

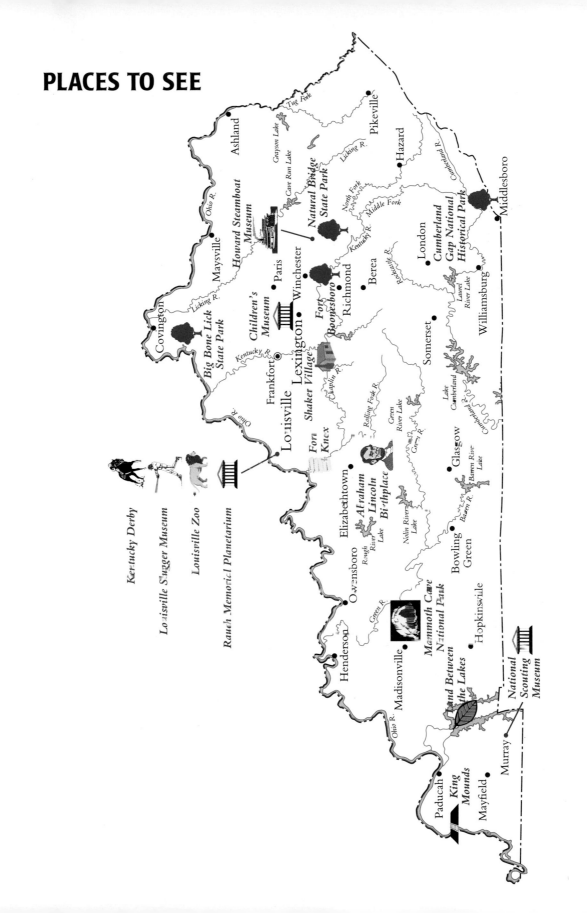

Pikeville

Ashland

Hazard

Middlesboro

Howard Steamboat Museum

Natural Bridge State Park

Maysville

Paris

Winchester

London

Cumberland Gap National Historical Park

Covington

Children's Museum

Fort Boonesboro

Berea

Richmond

Williamsburg

Big Bone Lick State Park

Lexington

Shaker Village

Somerset

Frankfort

Louisville

Fort Knox

Kentucky Derby

Louisville Slugger Museum

Louisville Zoo

Rauch Memorial Planetarium

Abraham Lincoln Birthplace

Elizabethtown

Glasgow

Owensboro

Bowling Green

Henderson

Madisonville

Mammoth Cave National Park

Hopkinsville

Land Between the Lakes

National Scouting Museum

Murray

Paducah

King Mounds

Mayfield

Rivers and lakes labeled on map: Tug Fork, Grayson Lake, Licking R., Cumberland R., Cave Run Lake, Ohio R., North Fork, Middle Fork, Kentucky R., Rockcastle R., Licking R., Laurel River Lake, Kentucky R., Chaplin R., Rolling Fork R., Green River Lake, Lake Cumberland, Green R., Barren River Lake, Barren R., Cumberland, Nolin River Lake, Rough River Lake, Green R., Ohio R.

On most days, a rainbow graces Cumberland Falls.

exhibits on everything from the Adena culture to the development of radio. It also houses a great collection of antique clothing.

The arts flourish in eastern Kentucky, particularly in Berea, which is known as Kentucky's crafts capital. The town is famous for its basket making, textiles, pottery, and woodworking. At Berea College, instructors keep old traditions alive while also teaching students modern styles.

Many people have seen a rainbow. But few have seen a moon-bow, unless they have traveled to eastern Kentucky's Cumberland Falls. When the conditions are just right, the light of the full moon strikes the mist of the waterfall to create a moonbow. This wondrous phenomenon does not occur anywhere else in the Western Hemisphere.

Cumberland Falls is the second-largest waterfall east of the Rocky Mountains. It is 125 feet wide and falls 68 feet. Several well-marked trails give visitors spectacular views of the falls, which always has a rainbow arching out of it except on the cloudiest days. To get a real feel for the power of the water, a guide will row you upriver to the very base of the falls. Everyone in the boat gets drenched by the pounding spray thrown up as the water hits the river, and conversation is impossible in the roar of the water.

Ian James, who pilots boats to the falls, is quick to point out the power of the water. "A few years ago," he recalls, "a man was out fishing and fell asleep in his boat. He woke up as it was going over the falls. He was pretty banged up, but he lived. A college girl who was wading and was swept away by the current wasn't so lucky."

THE HEART OF KENTUCKY

You don't have to be a horse lover to enjoy the beautiful Bluegrass Region; they say that if you don't love horses when you go to the Bluegrass, you will by the time you leave! But central Kentucky has more than thoroughbreds. The world's largest cave system, exciting cities, beautiful rivers, and wonderful parks are all to be found in Kentucky's heartland.

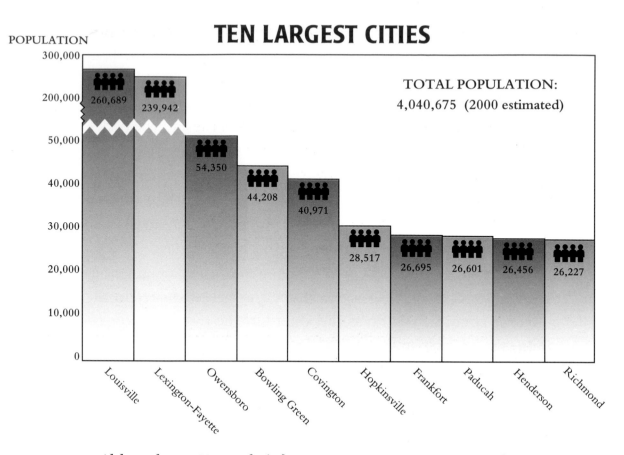

TEN LARGEST CITIES

POPULATION

300,000

200,000

50,000

40,000

30,000

20,000

10,000

0

TOTAL POPULATION:
4,040,675 (2000 estimated)

260,689 — Louisville
239,942 — Lexington-Fayette
54,350 — Owensboro
44,208 — Bowling Green
40,971 — Covington
28,517 — Hopkinsville
26,695 — Frankfort
26,601 — Paducah
26,456 — Henderson
26,227 — Richmond

Although not Kentucky's largest city, Lexington attracts the most visitors. Founded in 1775, Lexington was once known as the Athens of the West because of its wealth and many cultural attractions. The city is still a center of art and history. The Kentucky Gallery of Fine Crafts and Art showcases local craftspeople and artists, and ArtsPlace also concentrates on Kentucky artists.

Not all of Lexington's museums are devoted to culture. The Lexington Children's Museum is one of the most visited children's museums in the country. The museum encourages visitors to touch, play, and explore with such displays as a giant human heart that you can walk through and a hands-on exhibit that shows how to create animation.

There's no doubt about it, horses are the major attraction of central Kentucky. And there's no better place for the horse lover than the Kentucky Horse Park. Located north of the city, the park is the Bluegrass Region's most popular tourist attraction. People visit the park to see beautiful bronze statues of famous racehorses, including a huge statue of the most famous racehorse of all time, Man o' War, and to watch shows featuring more than forty breeds

The Kentucky Horse Park includes a museum covering every aspect of horses as well as exhibitions featuring live animals.

of horses. Special shows are held throughout the year. For example, in the spring and summer, visitors are treated to the sight of the newborn foals with their mothers. Knowledgeable guides talk about the special bonds between mothers and foals.

The International Museum of the Horse provides much information for the curious. You can learn the history and characteristics of breeds, find out about the evolution of the horse from its earliest ancestors, and see examples of different sports involving horses. The Kentucky Horse Center is not just a spot to see horses—it is also a working thoroughbred training center where hundreds of animals are housed and trained.

The almost-vanished way of life of the Shakers can be seen at Shaker Village of Pleasant Hill. This religious community was founded in 1809 and operated for about a hundred years. United by their belief in simple living and their devotion to God, community, and hard work, the Shakers attempted to remove themselves from the rest of society and live in self-supporting communities. In the 1830s, about five hundred Shakers lived and worked at Pleasant Hill. The Shakers were renowned for their simple yet exquisite crafts. For instance, fabrics were sewn together so carefully that seams were hard to see. Today, you can tour Pleasant Hill's thirty buildings and watch craftspeople use traditional Shaker tools to demonstrate how the Shakers made their beautiful furniture, brooms, and cloth.

Kentucky's largest city, Louisville, is located in the central section of the state. The city was named for the French king Louis XVI in gratitude for his help to the young United States during the American Revolution. Although most famous as the site of the

At Pleasant Hill, the stunning simplicity of the buildings offers a picture of Shaker ideals.

WORK IS WORSHIP

The Shakers believed that work is worship, and that doing any less than your best when you work is an insult to God. This accounts for their products' durability, as well as their practicality and beauty.

Shakers are credited with the invention of the flat broom. Before this invention, a broom was nothing but a tightly tied bundle of straw. The flat broom makes it easier to clean into corners and is more durable than the earlier type of broom. The Shakers were also the first to package seeds in envelopes, which were cheaper to manufacture and easier to ship than the boxes in which seeds had been sold earlier.

The Shakers often made ingenious labor-saving devices. The houses at Pleasant Hill have many pegs on the walls. Everything that could be hung up was suspended from one of these pegs—when someone was finished with a chair, up it went on the wall. Brooms, ladders, and other tools had handles that could hook onto the pegs. Because everything was hung up, floors could be swept very quickly.

Louisville is Kentucky's largest city.

Kentucky Derby, Louisville is rich in history and other attractions. Visitors can enjoy trips to the orchestra, opera, ballet, and theater.

Louisville's early prosperity came from the Ohio River, and the river still plays an important role there. Visitors can view the city in one of the world's oldest operating steamboats, the *Belle of Louisville*. The boat looks much the same today as it did when it began cruising the Ohio in 1914.

The Belle of Louisville *brings a touch of the past to the Ohio River.*

While horse fans know Louisville as the home of the Kentucky Derby, baseball fans have another association with the city: the Louisville Slugger, the most famous baseball bat in the world, is made there. The Louisville Slugger factory supplies three-quarters of all the baseball bats for the professional teams in the United States. Many major-league players travel to Louisville to personally pick out the wood that will be used for their bats, and to try out new shapes and sizes.

The Louisville Slugger Museum is a treasure trove for anyone who loves America's national sport. It is easy to spot—the world's

It's hard to miss Louisville's bat museum.

largest bat looks like it's leaning on the building. This 120-foot-tall steel structure is supported only at its base—it does not touch the building itself. "If there's ever a tornado, we're in trouble," jokes one of the tour guides. Rare and historic baseball memorabilia are on display there, and you can tour a locker room and a dugout. You can also see how baseball bats are made, starting in the forest and winding up at home plate.

South of Louisville is Fort Knox, where some of the gold belonging to the U.S. government is stored. As you can imagine, security at Fort Knox is very strict. In fact, visitors are not even allowed. It is such a safe storage area that in addition to gold, other precious items have been stored there. During World War II, original copies of the Declaration of Independence, the United States Constitution, and the Gettysburg Address were kept in vaults at Fort Knox.

One of the world's greatest natural wonders is in central Kentucky. Mammoth Cave is the longest known cave system in the world, with over 350 miles of mapped trails. Prehistoric people knew about this cave and mined minerals from it. Bodies of prehistoric people have been found in the cave, along with artifacts such as spearheads and sandals. These peoples stopped using the cave about two thousand years ago. After it was rediscovered in the nineteenth century, the cave quickly became a fashionable spot to visit. Slaves would guide tourists through with lanterns and smoky torches. Today, the half-million visitors who tour the cave each year can still see where some of these early tourists wrote their names on the ceiling with soot from the torches.

Since there is no light deep in the cave, strange animals have

At Mammoth Cave, today's tourists can see where visitors from a century ago wrote their names in soot on the ceiling.

evolved in its depths. Eyeless fish, shrimp, and crayfish swim in the cave's pools, while eyeless beetles crawl along the walls and floors. Many of these animals have lost their coloration and look white or pink. These shy animals usually hide from visitors, but it is estimated that 130 species spend at least part of their lives in

Mammoth Cave. Some of them have been found nowhere else in the world.

In a few places in the cave, water constantly drips through the ceiling. Each drop leaves behind a tiny trace of minerals. Over thousands of years, the bits of minerals accumulate into stalagmites, towering formations that rise from the floor where the water hit, and stalactites, spikes that come down from the ceiling. Some have developed into unusual shapes, and if you use your imagination you can see faces, animals, and other forms in them.

Not far from Mammoth Cave, near Hodgenville, is the birthplace of President Abraham Lincoln. A log cabin similar to the one in which he was born sits on top of a hill near the stream where the Lincoln family got its water. Measuring only twelve by seventeen feet, the modest cabin has only one door and one window. But in the early nineteenth century, it was considered a good home.

WESTERN KENTUCKY

The long, narrow piece of land that is western Kentucky has some of the state's most beautiful wildlife. But don't forget to visit the many historic landmarks that are found there.

The great American art form, the patchwork quilt, has its most important museum in Paducah. Visitors come from all over the world to admire these magnificent creations in the Museum of the American Quilter's Society and to participate in the National Quilt Show. Patchwork quilts are made from small pieces of fabric sewn together in patterns and then attached to a backing by a pattern of stitches called "quilting." Most of the examples in the

Artisans at Homeplace demonstrate traditional crafts such as these dolls carved from wood.

show are considered works of art and are never used as bedspreads.

Land Between the Lakes National Recreation Area, on the border with Tennessee, opened in 1963. At the park, visitors learn about pre–Civil War farm life at the Homeplace, sixteen log buildings where early-nineteenth-century crafts are demonstrated. Blacksmiths make horseshoes, people stir bubbling pots full of liquid soap, and whittlers carve charming figures out of wood. Rare and

Bison roam the fields at the Land Between the Lakes National Recreation Area.

endangered animals can be seen at the park's Nature Station. But the park's most spectacular wild animals are the elk and bison that have been reintroduced into the area. Small herds of bison now roam the same fields where they were once plentiful.

Kentucky's wildlife has fascinated people for centuries. The illustrator John James Audubon lived in Henderson between 1810 and 1819, observing the birds that he would later gain fame for painting. The woods where he wandered have been turned into the

John James Audubon State Park, which now contains a museum showing many of his lifelike paintings as well as some of his journals and letters.

Humorist Irvin S. Cobb said in 1924, "A Kentuckian stays put." Travel through the Bluegrass State, and you might be tempted to stay put too.

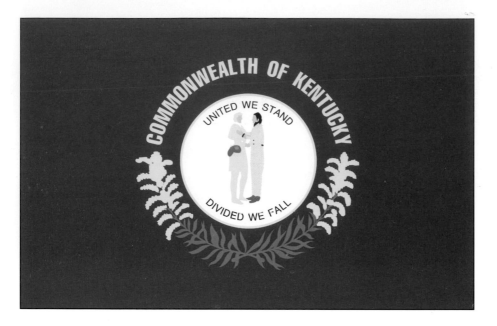

THE FLAG: *Adopted in 1918, the flag shows the state seal on a field of blue, surrounded by the words "Commonwealth of Kentucky" above and a wreath of goldenrod below.*

THE SEAL: *Adopted in 1918, the state seal depicts a frontiersman in buckskin shaking hands with a statesman dressed in a tailcoat. This symbolizes the relationship between Kentucky–the first "western" state–and its neighbors to the east. The two figures are encircled by the state motto, "United We Stand, Divided We Fall."*

STATE SURVEY

Statehood: June 1, 1792

Origin of Name: Probably derives from the Cherokee word *Kentahteh*, variously translated as "land of tomorrow," "land where we live," "meadow land," or "place of old fields." The name is also attributed to Iroquois and Wyandot words meaning "prairie" or "cane and turkey lands."

Nickname: Bluegrass State

Capital: Frankfort

Motto: United We Stand, Divided We Fall

Bird: Cardinal

Animal: Gray squirrel

Horse: Thoroughbred horse

Fish: Kentucky bass

Cardinal

MY OLD KENTUCKY HOME

Since before the Civil War, the estate of Federal Hill, near Bardstown, has been known as the Old Kentucky Home. The name became attached to it because Stephen Foster may have composed "My Old Kentucky Home" there in 1852. In 1928, Foster's composition became the official state song.

Words and Music by Stephen Foster

The sun shines bright on my old Ken-tuck-y home, 'Tis
young folks roll on the lit-tle cab-in floor, All

sum-mer, the peo-ple are gay. The corn top's ripe and the
mer-ry, all hap-py and bright. By'n bye hard times comes a-

1.
mead-ow's in bloom, While the birds make mu-sic all the day. The
knock-ing at the door, Then my

2.
old Ken-tuck-y home, good-night.

Chorus
Weep no more, my

la-dy, Oh! weep no more to-day. We will sing one song for my

old Ken-tuck-y home, For my old Ken-tuck-y home far a-way.

Insect: Viceroy butterfly

Flower: Goldenrod

Tree: Kentucky coffee tree

Mineral: Freshwater pearl

Soil: Crider soil series

Fossil: Brachiopod

GEOGRAPHY

Highest Point: 4,145 feet above sea level, at Black Mountain in Harlan County

Lowest Point: 257 feet above sea level, in southwestern Fulton County at the Mississippi River

Area: 40,410 square miles

Greatest Distance, North to South: 180 miles

Greatest Distance, East to West: 425 miles

Bordering States: Ohio, Indiana, and Illinois to the north, West Virginia and Virginia to the east, Tennessee to the south, and Missouri to the west

Hottest Recorded Temperature: 114°F on July 28, 1930 at Greensburg

Coldest Recorded Temperature: -34°F on January 19, 1994 at Shelbyville

Average Annual Precipitation: 48 inches

Major Rivers: Barren, Big Sandy, Cumberland, Dix, Green, Kentucky, Licking, Mississippi, Nolin, Ohio, Rockcastle, Rolling Fork, Salt, Tennessee, Tradewater, Tug

Major Lakes: Barkley, Barren, Buckhorn, Cave Run, Dewey, Fishtrap, Green, Herrington, Kentucky, Nolin, Reelfoot, Roughrider

Trees: ash, bald cypress, beech, buckeye, eastern red cedar, elm, hemlock, hickory, holly, linden, locust, maple, northern white cedar, oak, pine, sassafras, sweet and black gum, sycamore, tulip poplar, walnut

Wild Plants: azalea, bloodroot, bluebell, bluegrass, buttercup, fringed gentian, ginseng, goldenrod, jack-in-the-pulpit, kudzu, mayapple, mountain laurel, pennyroyal, rhododendron, trillium, violet, watermeal

Animals: black bear, fox, mink, mouse, opossum, raccoon, river otter, shrew, skunk, squirrel, white-tailed deer, wild boar, wildcat

Wild boar

Birds: bald eagle, blue jay, brown thresher, cardinal, catbird, chickadee, crested flycatcher, dove, duck, goose, grouse, hawk, osprey, owl, pheasant, quail, robin, slate-colored junco, sparrow, starling, towhee, tufted titmouse, wild turkey, yellow-bellied sapsucker

Fish: bass, bluegill, catfish, crappie, drum, jack salmon, rainbow trout, sauger, sucker, walleye, white perch

Endangered Animals: American peregrine falcon, bald eagle, blackside dace, clubshell, fanshell, fat pocketbook, gray bat, Indiana bat, Kentucky cave shrimp, least tern, northern riffleshell, palezone shiner, pallid sturgeon, pearly mussel, pink ring mussel, piping plover, red-cockaded woodpecker, relic darter, tan riffleshell, Virginia big-eared bat, winged mapleleaf mussel

Red-cockaded woodpecker

Endangered Plants: Cumberland rosemary, Cumberland sandwort, Price's potato-bean, running buffalo clover, Short's goldenrod, Virginia spiraea, white-haired goldenrod

TIMELINE

Kentucky History

1600s The Cherokee, Chickasaw, Wyandot, Delaware, and Shawnee tribes use the region as a hunting ground

1750 Dr. Thomas Walker becomes the first European to cross the Cumberland Gap, which he names

1767 Daniel Boone enters and explores the region

1774 Virginia defeats the Cherokee, Chickasaw, Wyandot, Delaware, and Shawnee tribes and forces them to sign a treaty giving up all rights to lands south of the Ohio River

1774 James Harrod founds Kentucky's first permanent settlement, Harrodsburg

1775 Daniel Boone founds Fort Boonesborough on the south bank of the Kentucky River

1776 Kentucky officially becomes the region's name when it becomes a county of Virginia

1778–1779 During the American Revolution, General George Rogers Clark defeats Indian, French, and British forces at Vincennes

1782 Indians defeat settlers at Blue Licks, the last major Indian battle in the region

1792 Kentucky becomes the 15th state

1809 Abraham Lincoln is born on February 12 in a log cabin near Hodgenville

1849 Kentuckian Zachary Taylor becomes the 12th president of the United States

1861 State is deeply divided by the Civil War; 70,000 men enlist with the Union forces and 35,000 men with the Confederates

1865–1870 Following the Civil War, industry thrives but many farmers are bankrupted by financial panics

1875 First Kentucky Derby is run at Churchill Downs

1891 Third and present state constitution adopted

1899 After a contested election for governor, the declared winner is shot and killed. His successor and opponent vie for power, which almost erupts into a civil war.

1905–1909 During the so-called Black Patch War, bands of night-riding terrorists try to force tobacco farmers into joining cooperatives

1930s Many strikes in the coal fields erupt in violence between strikers and armed guards hired by the coal companies; the Great Depression drives many farmers off their land to seek employment in urban areas

1941–1945 World War II brings a boom to the state's mining and manufacturing industries, as factories produce war materials

1945 Opening of interstate highways and four-lane toll roads connects isolated sections of the state

1954 The public school system is desegregated

1960 Kentucky passes strict laws requiring mining companies to restore and reforest strip-mine pits

1966 Kentucky is the first southern state to pass a comprehensive civil rights law

1970 Majority of population of the state is urban rather than rural for the first time

1983 Martha Layne Collins is elected the state's first woman governor

1987 Toyota builds a giant auto manufacturing plant near Georgetown, bringing many jobs to the state and leading other auto manufacturers to follow

1990 State supreme court declares the state's public school system unconstitutional and orders the General Assembly to create a new system which distributes educational funds fairly between rural and urban districts

1996 National Education Association rates Kentucky's schools among the top three in the nation

ECONOMY

Agricultural Products: beef cattle, corn, forest products, hay, horses, poultry, silk, soybeans, tobacco

Beef cattle

Manufactured Products: chemicals, electronics, food processing, metalworking, petrochemicals, pottery and glass products, textiles, tobacco products, transportation equipment, whiskey

Natural Resources: coal, natural gas, oil, stone

Business and Trade: construction, finance, insurance, printing and publishing, real estate, tourism, transportation

CALENDAR OF CELEBRATIONS

National All-Region Finals Rodeo See real cowboys in action every February as Bowling Green hosts the 20 top rodeo competitors in the world in seven events, including cattle roping and branding, bucking broncos, and fancy horseback riding.

Humana Festival of New American Plays From late February through March in Louisville, this renowned festival offers you a chance to see world premiers of new plays. In past years the festival has featured plays by such internationally recognized writers as Beth Henley, John Guare, Athol Fugard, Wole Soyinka, Jimmy Breslin, Harry Crews, Marsha Norman, Arthur Kopit, Joyce Carol Oates, Lanford Wilson, and Tony Kushner.

The Paducah Dogwood Trail Celebration Each April, visitors to Paducah are invited to travel a 12-mile trail to admire the blooms of these beautiful pink flowering trees.

Kentucky Derby On the first Saturday in May every year since 1875, huge crowds have turned out to cheer on their favorite horses and jockeys at this internationally famous horse race at Churchill Downs in Louisville.

The Mountain Laurel Festival Pine Mountains State Resort Park near Pineville hosts this annual mid-May festival. Come admire the laurel blossoms as you walk the park's nature trails. Then linger to browse and buy mountain handicrafts on display by local artists and craftspeople.

Highland Games Each June this festival of Scottish traditions at Glasgow features athletic events, such as the caber toss and the stone throw, plus traditional and contemporary Scottish music.

Boone Day Every June in Frankfort the Kentucky Historical Society commemorates the day Daniel Boone first entered Kentucky by staging a parade and historical reenactments.

Official Kentucky State Championship Old-Time Fiddlers Contest You'll have trouble keeping your toes from tapping as the best musicians from around the country compete in 15 categories of old-time and bluegrass fiddle music every July in Falls of Rough.

The 450-Mile Outdoor Sale Gas up the car, put some money in your pocket, and visit the world's longest outdoor sale, which stretches from Covington, Kentucky, to Gadsden, Alabama, along historic U.S. Route 127. Every August, this shoppers' bonanza offers antiques, quilts, arts and crafts, furniture, music, and a variety of handcrafted and homemade items.

Kentucky State Fair More than 600,000 people turn out each August at the Louisville State Fairgrounds for such events as the World's Championship Horse Show, rooster-crowing contests, pig races, and performances by top-name music acts.

Bluegrass Music Festival of the United States Bring your dancing shoes or just relax in the sun on Labor Day weekend as Louisville celebrates the

*Period costumes
in Perryville*

state's own homegrown brand of music with one of the largest free bluegrass music events in the country. Hear the best performers in the country on the guitar, banjo, dulcimer, fiddle, mandolin, and autoharp.

Festival of the Horse This annual mid-September event in Georgetown features exhibits involving everything you can possibly imagine relating to horses, plus arts and crafts and music.

Trail of Tears Indian Powwow This Native American gathering each September in Hopkinsville commemorates the 1838 forced removal of the Cherokees from their lands to reservations in Oklahoma. Everyone is welcome at this giant display of Native American dancing, crafts, and storytelling.

North American International Livestock Expo Travel to Louisville in November to see hordes of handsome cattle, horses, swine, sheep, and goats at one of the largest livestock shows in the world. More than $5 million dollars in prizes are awarded every year.

My Old Kentucky Home Candlelight Tours View 19th-century holiday decorations—yule logs, candlelit trees, paper angels, and homemade candles as musicians and carolers entertain in November and December in this famous Bardstown home.

Appalachian Christmas Arts and Crafts Market Artists and craftspeople display their quilts, crockery, carvings, embroidery, knitting, musical instruments, paintings, and drawings in Morehead during December.

The Shaker Order of Christmas Shaker holiday traditions and music are on display at Pleasant Hill during December. Hear—and dance to—Shaker hymns. Sample the simple, rich, and delicious Shaker cooking.

STATE STARS

Muhammad Ali (1942–   ) was born Cassius Clay in Louisville. He was the gold medal winner in boxing at the 1960 Olympics and became the boxing World Heavyweight Champion in 1964. The title was taken from him in 1967 when he was convicted of draft evasion for refusing to serve in the army for religious reasons. Following a Supreme Court ruling that overturned his conviction, Ali regained his title in 1974. Ali's engaging personality and passionate involvement in the civil rights movement brought him fame outside the ring. Although he retired from boxing in 1981, he remains one of the world's most popular sports figures.

John James Audubon (1785–1851) was born in Haiti but came to Kentucky as a youth. Audubon was a naturalist who specialized in the study of birds. His drawings and paintings of birds in their natural habitats brought him worldwide acclaim for their beauty, as well as for their scientific detail and accuracy.

John James Audubon

Ned Beatty (1937–   ), a popular movie and television actor, was born in a suburb of Louisville. He is best known for his role in the film *Deliverance* and for his Academy Award–nominated performance in *Network*. He was also nominated for an Emmy for his performance in the television movie *Friendly Fire*.

Daniel Boone (1734–1820) was one of the first whites to explore and settle in Kentucky. Boone gained a reputation as a valiant frontiersman. When his daughter was kidnapped by Indians in 1776, he led a party that followed and fought the Indians and returned her unharmed. Boone himself was captured by Indians several times and escaped each time—once making a long, hazardous journey to warn the inhabitants of Boonesborough, a settlement he had founded, of an impending attack.

Louis Brandeis (1856–1941) was born in Louisville. He served for 23 years on the U.S. Supreme Court, from 1916 to 1939, where he fought to protect individual liberties. Brandeis, the first Jewish Supreme Court justice, is considered one of the greatest legal scholars to ever sit on the Court.

William Wells Brown (1814–1884) was born a slave in Lexington. After gaining his freedom, he became a writer and abolitionist leader. He wrote what is believed to be the first novel, the first travel book, and the first play to be published by an African American.

Christopher "Kit" Carson (1809–1868), the famous western trapper and guide, was born in Madison County. Carson traveled all across the American West and Southwest. He accompanied John C. Fremont on various journeys of exploration in the Rocky Mountains region from 1842 through 1846. He fought for the Union during the Civil War and attained the rank of brigadier general.

Christopher "Kit" Carson

Albert Benjamin (Happy) Chandler (1898–1991) was a popular public official and sports figure. He served two terms as governor and one as U.S. senator. A former professional baseball player and coach, he was named commissioner of baseball in 1945. Professional baseball was desegregated during Chandler's term as commissioner. In 1982 he was elected to the National Baseball Hall of Fame. Chandler was born in Corydon.

Cassius Marcellus Clay (1810–1903) was born in Madison County. He served in the Kentucky legislature and published an abolitionist newspaper in Lexington. In 1856 he was one of the founders of the Republican Party. In 1861 President Abraham Lincoln appointed him ambassador to Russia.

Henry Clay (1777–1852) was born in Virginia but settled in Kentucky in 1787. As a U.S. senator he was known as the Great Compromiser for his work on the Missouri Compromise. He was secretary of state under President John Quincy Adams and served in the U.S. Senate on three separate occasions.

John Colgan (1840–1916) a druggist from Louisville, was the inventor of the first chewing gum, Colgan's Taffy Tolu, which gained widespread popularity after it was introduced at the 1893 Chicago world's fair.

Martha Layne Collins (1936–   ) was the first female governor of Kentucky, serving from 1983 through 1987. She was born in Shelby County and first attracted public attention as a teen when she was selected as Queen of the Kentucky Derby. Before becoming involved in politics, she was a junior high school teacher. As governor, Collins was noted for her reform of the state's educational system and for attracting new businesses to the state.

Billy Ray Cyrus (1961–   ) was born in Flatlands and was one of the best-

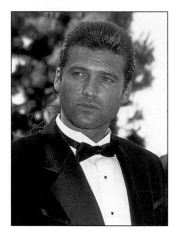

selling country singing stars of the 1990s. His string of popular hits includes "Achy Breaky Heart," "It's All the Same to Me," "Trail of Tears," "Could've Been Me," and "Words By Heart."

Billy Ray Cyrus

Jefferson Davis (1808–1889) was the first and only president of the Confederate States of America. He was born in Elkton, graduated from the U.S. military academy at West Point, and then served in the army in various posts in the West. Davis became a U.S. senator from Mississippi in 1845, served as U.S. secretary of war from 1853 to 1857, and then returned to the Senate. Davis worked to maintain the Union until Mississippi seceded in 1861, when he reluctantly resigned his Senate seat. Following the Confederate defeat, Davis was imprisoned for two years for treason against the U.S. government.

Lionel Hampton (1913–   ), an internationally celebrated jazz vibraphonist, drummer, and bandleader, was born in Louisville. Hampton was the first significant player of the jazz vibraphone. He played with Benny Goodman from 1936 to 1940, and then left to build his own band.

Lionel Hampton

Naomi (1946–   ) and **Wynonna** (1964–   ) **Judd** were both born in Ashland. As the popular mother-daughter singing duo, the Judds, they won the Country Music Association award for Vocal Group of the Year every year from 1985 through 1992. In 1993, after health reasons stopped Naomi from performing, Wynonna went solo and won the Best Female Vocalist of the Year award. Among the Judds' hits are "She Is His Only Need," "I Saw the Light," "My Strongest Weakness," and "Love Can Build a Bridge."

Abraham Lincoln (1809–1865), the 16th president of the United States, was born in a log cabin on his father's homestead near Hodgenville. His family moved to Indiana when he was 7 and to Illinois when he was 21. His early education was slight; as an adult he estimated that his total formal schooling amounted to less than one year. Nevertheless, Lincoln became a lawyer. After serving in the Illinois House of Representatives and the U.S. Senate, in 1860 he was elected president. He led the nation through the Civil War but was assassinated shortly after the war ended.

Loretta Lynn (1935–   ) has had a long career as one of the most popular female country music singers in the nation. Lynn was born into a poor coal miner's family in Butcher Hollow. Her autobiography, *Coal Miner's Daughter*, was made into a very successful movie. Among her best-known songs are "You Ain't Woman Enough," "Don't Come Home a' Drinkin'," and "Coal Miner's Daughter."

Loretta Lynn

Bobbie Ann Mason (1940–   ), born in Mayfield, is a novelist and short story writer best known for her novels *In Country*, *Feather Crowns*, and *Spence and Lila*. Her short story collection *Shiloh and Other Stories* won the Ernest Hemingway Award in 1983. *In Country* was made into a movie in 1988.

Thomas Merton (1915–1968) was a Trappist monk and a widely published writer and poet who spent most of his adult life at the monastery at Gethsemane, Kentucky. His early autobiography, *Seven Story Mountain*, was a national best-seller. More than 40 books followed on the subjects of peace, poverty, and social justice.

Bill Monroe (1911–1996), known as the Father of Bluegrass Music, was born on a farm just outside of Rosine. Monroe combined traditional Appalachian music with gospel and blues to create a new type of music, which came to be called "bluegrass" after his band, the Blue Grass Boys. In 1970 Monroe was inducted into the Country Music Hall of Fame, and in 1986 the U.S. Senate honored him with a special resolution praising his contributions to American music.

Carrie Nation (1846–1911), a leader of the American temperance movement, was born in Garrard County. Nation was famous for her hatchet-wielding raids on saloons. Her activities led to her arrest more than 30 times in various cities across the country.

Carrie Nation

Patricia Neal (1926–   ) is an internationally acclaimed stage and screen actress who was born in Packard. In 1963 she won an Oscar for Best Actress for the movie *Hud*.

Marsha Norman (1947–   ) won a Pulitzer Prize for her play *'Night, Mother* in 1983 and a Tony Award for the 1991 musical *The Secret Garden*. Most of Norman's plays have premiered at the Humana Festival of New American Plays in Louisville, which is where she was born.

Adolph Rupp (1910–1977) was the head coach of the record-setting University of Kentucky from 1930 to 1972. He led his teams to national championships in 1948, 1949, 1951, and 1958 and compiled a record of 876 wins during his long career.

Colonel Harland Sanders (1890–1980), using a special method of pressure cooking and several secret ingredients, built the Kentucky Fried Chicken restaurant chain from a single small café in Corbin to a multi-million dollar franchise business with branches all across the country and in several foreign countries.

Diane Sawyer (1945–   ), a nationally recognized television news journalist, was born in Glasgow. Sawyer was the first female reporter on the CBS news program *60 Minutes*. Currently, she is the host of ABC's *Primetime Live*.

Phillip A. Sharp (1944–   ) won the Nobel Prize in medicine and physiology in 1993 for the discovery of split genes and for advancing research on cancer and hereditary diseases. He was born in Falmouth.

Jesse Hilton Stuart (1906–1984), a popular author, was famous for his novels, short stories, and poems featuring his beloved Kentucky hill country. In 1980 Stuart donated 700 acres of land—all land his parents had worked as tenant farmers—to the state as a nature preserve.

Zachary Taylor (1784–1850), the 12th president of the United States, grew up in Jefferson County. He served with distinction in the War of 1812 and became a national hero for his successful conduct of the Mexican War. He became president in 1849 but died after only serving 16 months in office.

Robert Penn Warren (1905–1989), who was born in Guthrie, won the Pulitzer Prize for his novel *All the King's Men* in 1947. In 1957, he again won the Pulitzer and the National Book Award for his volume of poetry *Promises*. In 1986 Warren was appointed the first official poet laureate of the United States.

Whitney M. Young Jr. (1921–1971), born in Lincoln Ridge, was a leader in the civil rights movement. He helped build the National Urban League into one of the leading U.S. civil rights organizations. He served as its director from 1961 to 1971. He was a close advisor to President Lyndon Johnson and served on several presidential commissions.

TOUR THE STATE

Churchill Downs (Louisville) This one-mile oval track has been the home of the Kentucky Derby since 1875. The grounds are also the site of a museum of Derby history.

Louisville Slugger Museum (Louisville) This museum of baseball memorabilia is marked by a 120-foot, 68,000-pound steel baseball bat. The museum is adjacent to the Hillerich & Bradsby Company factory, where the world-famous baseball bats are manufactured.

Fort Knox (Fort Knox) holds much of the U.S. gold reserve. In addition to the country's gold supply, the bomb-proof building has at times held the British Crown Jewels, the Magna Carta, the United States Constitution, and the Declaration of Independence.

Kentucky Horse Park (Lexington) This thousand-acre park includes the International Museum of the Horse, which depicts the history of all breeds of horses.

Mary Todd Lincoln House (Lexington) The girlhood home of Abraham Lincoln's wife is a restored 1803 house containing period furniture and decorations from the Lincoln and Todd families.

Abraham Lincoln's boyhood home (Hodgenville)

Lexington Children's Museum (Lexington) This museum is the place for active, inquisitive kids. It features hands-on exhibits about science, nature, history, and ecology.

Nostalgia Station Toy and Train Museum (Versailles) A restored 1911 railroad station houses a model train display that is a treat for children of all ages. Exhibits include complete 1926 and 1950s Lionel train layouts with all the original accessories, as well as numerous children's toys and railroad memorabilia.

Shaker Village (Pleasant Hill) This restored Shaker village, which was founded in 1805, is the largest in the United States. The site contains many of the original living quarters, barns, and workshops.

Old Fort Harrod State Park (Harrodsburg) The park is on the land originally colonized by Captain James Harrod in 1774. From April to October, costumed staff portray the lives of the residents of the first permanent English settlement west of the Alleghenies.

Berea College Appalachian Museum (Berea) This museum brings to life the traditional Appalachian culture. Displays concern farming, blacksmithing, using vegetable dyes, and cooking over an open fire. Arts, crafts, and photos also illustrate the lifestyles of mountain people.

Daniel Boone National Forest (Winchester) Situated in rugged mountain country along the eastern border of the Bluegrass Region, this 690,000-acre forest features high sandstone cliffs, the Red River gorge, natural stone arches, waterfalls, and caves.

Fort Boonesboro State Park (Richmond) Artisans demonstrate 18th-century trades and skills in a re-creation of the fort built by Daniel Boone in 1775.

Cumberland Gap National Park (Middlesboro) This national historical park honors the pass through the Appalachian Mountains that served as a natural doorway for wildlife, explorers, and settlers. The park contains 55 miles of hiking trails through beautiful forested mountains.

Cumberland Falls (Corbin) This 125-foot-wide waterfall drops 68 feet into a boulder-strewn gorge of the Cumberland River. The water strikes with such force that a perpetual mist hovers over the valley, creating a "moonbow" on clear nights with a full moon.

My Old Kentucky Home State Park (Bardstown) It is believed that Stephen Foster wrote "My Old Kentucky Home" here in 1853 in the home that belonged to his cousin. The mansion is furnished with family heirlooms and portraits.

American Cave Museum (Horse Cave) This museum features displays on the region's caves and mines. Stairs lead down to an underground river that flows beneath the town of Horse Cave and was used to generate electricity in the 1800s.

Mammoth Cave National Park (Madisonville) Mammoth Cave, the longest known cave system in the world, became a national park in 1941. The explored portion of the cave covers 52,425 acres. Over three hundred miles of mapped underground corridors lead visitors past striking limestone, gypsum, and onyx formations, deep pits, and lofty domes.

Jefferson Davis Monument State Historical Site (Fairview) The 351-foot stone obelisk, one of the largest monuments in the United States, marks the birthplace of the president of the Confederate States of America. Visitors can ride an elevator to the top of the monument.

Land Between the Lakes National Recreation Area (Canton) In this wooded region between Barkley and Kentucky Lakes you can hike on more than 200 miles of trails and enjoy fishing, boating, swimming, and hunting. You might even see a buffalo herd.

National Scouting Museum (Murray) This museum on the campus of Murray State University chronicles the history of the Boy Scouts from 1910 to the present.

Museum of the American Quilter's Society (Paducah) The museum features exhibits of beautiful quilts, plus demonstrations of quilting and related crafts.

John James Audubon Museum and Nature Center (Henderson) This site features 435 original prints from the naturalist/illustrator's famous—and extremely valuable—1839 edition of his greatest work, *The Birds of America*. You can also see exhibits relating to Audubon's life and travels.

FUN FACTS

The average attendance at the Kentucky Derby is 130,000 people, which is amazing considering the stands at Churchill Downs only seat 48,000 people. Everyone else crowds into the infield and struggles to get a spot near the fence. The derby's largest attendance was 163,628 in 1974, the 100th running of the race. That year 23 horses entered—the largest number ever. The smallest number ever to run was three, in 1892 and in 1905.

Cumberland Falls is the only place in North America where you can see a "moonbow"—a rainbow caused by the light of the full moon shining though the mist of the falls.

FIND OUT MORE

If you want to learn more about Kentucky, check your local library or bookstore for these titles:

BOOKS

General State Books

Brown, Dottie. *Kentucky*. Minneapolis: Lerner, 1992.

Fradin, Dennis B. *Kentucky*. Chicago: Children's Press, 1993.

Kleber, John E., ed. *The Kentucky Encyclopedia*. Lexington: University Press of Kentucky, 1992.

Thompson, Kathleen. *Kentucky*. Austin, TX: Raintree Steck-Vaughn, 1996.

Special Interest Books

Cavan, Seamus. *Daniel Boone and the Opening of the Ohio Country*. New York: Chelsea House, 1991.

Conklin, Thomas. *Muhammad Ali: The Fight for Respect*. Brookfield, CT: Millbrook Press, 1991.

Hubbard-Brown, Janet. *The Shawnee*. New York: Chelsea House, 1995.

WEBPAGE

http://www.state.ky.us

CD-ROM

United States Geography: The Southeast. Chicago: Clearvue/eav.

VIDEOS

The Geography of the Southeastern States. Chicago: Society for Visual Education.

Looking for America: The Southeast. Chicago: Clearvue/eav.

SOFTWARE

Great American States Race. Broken Arrow, OK: Heartsoft.

INDEX

Chart, graph, and illustration page numbers are in boldface.